Abiezer Coppe
Selected Writings

A Fiery Flying Roll
A Remonstrance of the sincere and zealous
Protestation
Copp's Return to the wayes of Truth
Divine Fire-Works
A Character of a True Christian
◊

Appendix: Die Veneris, I Februarii, 1649

edited and introduced by Andrew Hopton

Aporia Press
London 1987

D1556071

Aporia Press, 308 Camberwell New Road, London SE5 ORW

British Library Cataloguing in Publication Data:
Coppe, Abiezer
Abiezer Coppe : selected writings.
1. Great Britain — History — Charles I,
1625-1649   2. Great Britain — History —
Commonwealth and protectorate, 1649-1660
I. Title   II. Hopton, Andrew
942.06'2   DA405

ISBN 0-948518-25-1

Set by Counter Productions
Printed by A. Wheaton & Co. Ltd., Exeter
Cover design by Edmund Baxter, incorporating an illustration from Coppe's
Divine Fire-works, reproduced by permission of the British Library.

INTRODUCTION

The Parliament voted that a Book written by one Coppe, intituled a fiery flying Roll, &c. contained many horrid blasphemies, and damnable Opinions, and that the Book and all Copies of it that can be found, shall be burnt by the hands of the Hangman[1].

THE PUBLICATION of Abiezer Coppe's *A Fiery Flying Roll* in January 1650 caused great controversy[2]. It led to Coppe being imprisoned and copies of the book being publicly burnt. It also prompted the government of the day to pass an Act of Parliament against 'Atheistical, Blasphemous and Execrable Opinions'. Coppe himself became something of a sensation and was the target of attacks by contemporary writers (many of whom chose to remain anonymous). It is clear that in his time Coppe received a great deal of attention. It is therefore somewhat surprising that until comparatively recently scholarship has virtually ignored him. In the last thirty years, however, the situation has changed and the publication of works by such eminent historians as Norman Cohn, A.L. Morton and Christopher Hill has done much to redress the balance[3]. Moreover the last five years has seen the publication of two important works on the subject - Nigel Smith's *A Collection of Ranter Writings* (which contains most of Coppe's writings together with works by his contemporaries) and J.C. Davis' *Fear, Myth and History*[4]. Until now, however, there has never been a volume devoted to Coppe alone (other than a facsimile of the *Fiery Flying Roll*) and it is with the intention of rectifying this situation that this publication is issued[5].

Included in this volume is Coppe's major work, the *Fiery Flying Roll*, together with the two pamphlets he issued from prison in order to expedite his release, *A Remonstrance of the sincere and zealous Protestation of Abiezer Coppe* and *Copp's Return to the wayes of Truth*. Two later works, *Divine Fire-works* and 'A Character of a true Christian', are reprinted here in their entirety for the first time. The parliamentary bill ordering all copies of the *Fiery Flying Roll* to be seized and burnt forms an appendix to this selection. The remainder of this introduction divides into two sections; *part ii* will attempt to place Coppe's work in its historical context and *part iii* will provide the reader with as much biographical detail as the scanty extant evidence will allow. I have avoided speculation and concentrated instead on collating data to enable readers to form their own conclusions in the light of Coppe's writings, upon which, necessarily, any interpretation must be based.

ABIEZER COPPE was writing at the time of the English Revolution. A new society was being shaped to replace that which had been destroyed by the Civil War (1642-49). It was a period which saw a great outpouring of radical ideas, political, religious and scientific. Publications were issued in their thousands, at a faster rate than at any previous time[6]. For a short time people were free to express themselves and to expound their ideas and visions of the form which the new society should take. England was in a state of political and religious expectation. With the execution of Charles I on the thirtieth of January 1649, the old order had been decisively swept away and it was felt by some that divine justice had been meted out. The opportunity to influence what was to replace the pre-revolutionary government inspired many groups and individuals to both action and debate. For a while these activities seemed to have had some influence on events: religious toleration prevailed, the army rank and file was to have a say in forming the constitution as a result of Leveller agitation. Gradually however, Cromwell and the army grandees, who represented the interests of the propertied, triumphed over egalitarian initiatives such as those proposed by the Levellers and Diggers. Society resumed its old hierarchical structure: social revolution was to go no further.

It was against this background of change and in this volatile atmosphere that Coppe's works appeared. He has often been described as a 'Ranter' and grouped together with other religious writers such as Joseph Salmon, Lawrence Clarkson (or Claxton) and Jacob Bauthumley[7]. In his recent and important work, however, J.C. Davis has demonstrated that there *was no* organised group, although some connections did exist between Coppe, Clarkson and Salmon, and that the term 'Ranter' was one applied by other writers at a later date[8]. Much of the literature which has been taken as evidence of a Ranter movement consists of a series of pamphlets which are the product of what would be described today as 'sensationalist journalism', and as early as the last century David Masson had observed:

> The pamphlets about them generally take the form of professed accounts of some of their meetings, with reports of their profane discourses and the indecencies with which they were accompanied. There are illustrative wood-cuts in some of the pamphlets; and, on the whole, I fancy that some low printers and booksellers made a trade on the public curiosity about the Ranters, getting up pretended accounts of their meetings as a pretext for prurient publications[9].

Several of these pamphlets paid particular attention to Coppe and Clarkson, inventing highly scurrilous accounts of their behaviour as can be seen in this extract from *The Routing Of The Ranters*:

> ...and their Ring-leader, Copp (when he was fitter to have gone to bed and slept, than to have spoken in a publick place) bestowed an hours time in belching forth imprecations, curses, and other such like stuffe, as is not fit to be once named amongst Christians: and when he perceived that he should be called to answer for the wicked blasphemies that he had uttered, at sundry times, he took two of his she-Disciples, and went to the Citie of Coventrie, where it was soon dispersed abroad, that he commonly lay in bed with two women at a time; whereof he being soberly admonished by an Officer of the army, he replied, that it was his libertie, and he might use it; saying further that unreasonable creatures are not restrained of it. With many other speeches to justifie himselfe in his ungodly practises, for which he was apprehended and brought up to London, and by the Magistrate committed to Newgate[10].

Coppe was later to complain about such treatment and to deny the truth of such accounts in his postscript to *A Remonstrance* (see below).

Davis has argued that the image of 'Ranterism' was used as 'a weapon with which serious and God-fearing men could fight the Good fight'[11]. The term 'Ranter' was a pejorative one used to describe those whose opinions were seen as extreme and dangerous by others who wished to dissociate themselves from such people and to appear more moderate in their own opinions. Davis further observes: 'Ranterism came to represent any anti-social manifestation of the light within' (God within man)[12]. To refer to someone as a 'Ranter' was not to identify them with any single coherent set of ideas or beliefs, nor any specific group of people, but to define them negatively for strategic reasons. The idea or image of the 'Ranter' was essentially a device employed by sensationalist pamphleteers to generate interest in their publications, and by Baptists, Quakers and other religious sects to distinguish themselves from what was seen by established Puritanism as the 'lunatic fringe'. It is evident therefore that it is insufficient merely to describe Coppe as a Ranter and, while it may give us an indication of the effect he had on his contemporaries, the term does nothing to elucidate his ideas or beliefs.

In order to understand what Coppe was trying to achieve we must rather turn our attention to the religious climate in which he was writing. The end of all hope of social revolution had not therefore meant an end to all religious expectation. In fact once all possibility of obtaining an egalitarian society by political means had been effectively removed, little hope remained *except* for divine intervention. Religious toleration had led to a greater circulation of ideas, ideas not necessarily new, but at least now openly expressed. The doctrines of Joachim of Fiore (1130-1200) were one such body of ideas which were influential at this time[13]. According to these beliefs, once the Anti-Christ had been defeated the world was to enter a new age of the spirit when man would reach perfection on earth: this was to be the age of the Everlasting Gospel, which A.L. Morton has described thus:

> In the coming age of the Spirit the full truth of the Everlasting Gospel will be revealed, not in a new sacred book but in a new revelation of the spiritual sense of the Bible with which God will illuminate the hearts of men. In this age God will be within man and therefore all existing forms of worship, ceremonies, churches, legal and moral codes will become superfluous. Instead of appearing as a force from without, God will now be within, and the unity of God and man will be fully accomplished[14].

The defeat of Charles I and the Royalists could be, and was, interpreted as the defeat of the Anti-Christ, and the expectation of entering into a new age was a theme common to many of the religious pamphlets of these times including Coppe's *Fiery Flying Roll*. This work, published within a year of the execution of King Charles, contains an attack on formalism and suggests that practical charity is the most important aspect of true Christianity. From this critical religious position, Coppe delivers an egalitarian social message, one which is informed in particular by the promise of the Joachite 'new age'. Davis has observed that

> Coppe's vision was ... of a soon to be purged and reformed society. The spirit of Christ would cast down the mighty and the wealthy, sweep away the hypocrisy of formal religion and open the hearts of

men and women to a life of true charity, of true righteousness[15].

It was an alarming message and all the more so since it could be argued from the teachings of Christ[16]. True Christianity, Coppe implied, undermined property and called for equality for *all* men (even the Levellers had excluded certain people, such as servants, from their demands for equality and had not questioned the sanctity of property). Such a message led to accusations of blasphemy, the banning and burning of the *Fiery Flying Roll* and Coppe's arrest and imprisonment. Coppe claimed that the Blasphemy Act of August 1650 was passed 'because of me'[17]. The contents of this act are worth reproducing at some length:

> The Parliament... finding to their great grief and astonishment, that there are divers men and women who have lately discovered themselves to be most monstrous in their Opinions, and loose in all wicked and abominable Practices hereafter mentioned, not onely to the notorious corrupting and disordering, but even to the dissolution of all Humane Society, who rejecting the use of any Gospel Ordinances, do deny the necessity of Civil and Moral Righteousness among men... all and every person and persons (not distempered with sickness, or distracted in brain) who shall presume avowedly in words to profess, or shall by writing proceed to affirm and maintain him or her self, or any other meer Creature, to be very God, or to be Infinitie or Almighty, or in Honor, Excellency, Majesty and Power to be equal, and the same with the true God, or that the true God, or the Eternal Majesty dwells in the Creature and no where else; or whosoever shall deny the Holiness and Righteousness of God, or shall presume as aforesaid to profess, That Unrighteousness, Prophane Swearing, Drunkenness, and the like Filthiness and Brutishness, are not wholy and forbidden in the Word of God, or that these acts in any person, or the persons [so] committing them, are approved of by God, or that such acts, or such persons in those things are like unto God: Or whosoever shall presume as aforesaid to profess, That these acts of Denying and Blaspheming God, or the Holiness or Righteousness of God; or the acts of cursing God, or of Swearing prophanely or falsely by the Name of God, or the acts of Lying, Stealing, Cousening and Defrauding others; or the acts of Murther, Adultery, Incest, Fornication, Uncleanness, Sodomy, Drunkenness, filthy and lascivious Speaking, are not things in themselves shameful, wicked, sinful, impious, abominable and detestable in any person... Or Whosoever shall avowedly as aforesaid profess, That whatsoever is acted by them (whether Whoredom, Adultery, Drunkenness or the like open Wickedness) may be committed without sin; or that such acts are acted by the true God, or by the Majesty of God, or the Eternity that is in them; That Heaven and all happiness consists in the acting of those things which are Sin and Wickedness; or that such men and women are most perfect, or like to God or Eternity, which do commit the greatest Sins with least remorse or sense; or that there is no such thing really and truly as Unrighteousness, Unholiness or Sin, but as a man or woman judgeth thereof; or that there is neither Heaven nor Hell... All and every person or persons so avowedly professing, maintaining or publishing as aforesaid, the aforesaid Atheistical Blasphemies or

Execrable Opinions... shall by the said Justice or Justices, or other Head-Officer committed to Prison or to the House of Correction, for the space of six moneths[18].

Coppe answered the charges against him in the pamphlets *A Remonstrance of the sincere and zealous Protestation of Abiezer Coppe* and *Copp's Return to the wayes of Truth*, both written in Newgate Gaol and published in 1651. In these works Coppe answered what he saw as false accusations (made both under the 'Blasphemy Act' and by sensationalist pamphlets such as those mentioned above), while at the same time he remained true to his social message[19]. Denying that he was guilty of sinning as charged, Coppe also emphasised that others were guilty of those sins which he saw as contrary to true Christianity. As Christopher Hill has observed, 'the sins he chose to stress were pride, covetousness, hypocrisy, oppression, tyranny, unmerciful-ness, despising the poor'[20].

Throughout all Coppe's works, the vision of an equal society founded on practical charity is the common theme. His writing is a step further in 'the search for a socially redemptive, practical Christianity, pursued before him by Levellers and Diggers'[21]. His message was not heeded, the 'new age of the spirit' never arrived, society remained as hierarchical as before. Within a decade of the publication of the *Fiery Flying Roll* the monarchy had been restored and the aspirations of the revolutionary period stifled. Instead of being hailed as a visionary, Coppe was branded a blasphemer and condemned to neglect. It is only recently that his work has at last been reappraised and its merits recognised. His writings are not only important for their social message and historical significance, but are also of considerable literary merit. The *Fiery Flying Roll* has been described by Hill as 'a powerful piece of writing, in a prose style unlike anything else in the seventeenth century'[22]. Work has been published suggesting links between Coppe's writings and those of Blake and comparing his work to that of Words-worth[23]. Whatever the validity of such speculations, it is clear from a reading of the *Fiery Flying Roll* that Coppe's is a unique and important achievement, and while the sense of urgency and violent passion which informs that piece may be absent from his lesser works, there too an element of intensity is often apparent. Coppe writes under the pressure of the imminence of apocalypse, desiring to express a broad vision but apparently obliged to use a condensed, abridged form: 'The time would faile if I would tell you all'. In this state of crisis, he seems able only to give hints (supported by numerous Biblical references) of what is to come: 'And this that is now (in this dead Letter hinted) is but the bare contents of some of those many things which the consuming fire is about to do these whipping times'. The writing tends to peter out, the urgency of Coppe's task preventing communication of anything but that which is essential, the repeated use of '&c.' prompting the reader to take up where it leaves off - to act: 'The End   Is not yet'. The insufficient 'dead letter' may still allow a tiny moment in which exists the possibility not for reflection so much as for change.

(iii)

THE SORT OF interpretation brought to bear on Coppe's writings is complemented by the various accounts of his life. When considering such accounts, it must be borne in mind that all the extant sources are biased in one way or another and that almost all are hostile. As Davis has pointed out:

> In 1650 Coppe was a sensation and he attracted the attention of sensation seekers. What he said and what others said about him must be sifted and weighed carefully[24].

Most of the sources of information about Coppe fall into three categories: sensationalist pamphlets such as those already mentioned; newsbook accounts which were usually biased according to their political viewpoint (for instance Royalist propaganda had a tendency to use figures such as Coppe as examples of the 'chaos' which existed in Commonwealth England); and finally, accounts in the writings of other contemporary religious figures (such as Richard Baxter and George Fox) whose comments were unsurprisingly biased in favour of their own particular religious perspective. Apart from these, the major source for details of Coppe's life is Anthony Wood's *Athenæ Oxonienses* which gives us an exaggerated and hostile account of Coppe's life and career but which is useful since it is the only account which relates some of the basic facts[25]. From these disparate sources it is possible to piece together a sketch of Coppe's life and career.

Abiezer Coppe was the son of Walter Coppe and was born in the borough of Warwick on the twentieth of May 1619. Other than what Coppe himself relates of his religious awakening at the age of thirteen in *Copp's Return to the wayes of Truth* (see below), nothing is known of his youth until he went to Oxford in early 1636, where he first attended All-Souls College, later to become postmaster at Merton. According to Wood (who relates the following anecdote) his behaviour at Oxford was infamous:

> And it was then notoriously known, that he would several times entertain for one night, or more, a wanton huswife in his chamber to whom carrying several times meat, at the hour of refection, he would make answer, when being asked by the way what he would do with it, that 'it was a bit for his cat'[26].

However, Wood was writing after Coppe's death and it is probable that this anecdote was concocted to justify Coppe's bad reputation and does not necessarily reflect the truth.

Coppe left university at the outbreak of the Civil War. At this time he appears to have been a Presbyterian but later he became an Anabaptist. He gained a considerable reputation as an Anabaptist preacher in the Warwick area (where, according to Wood he 'baptized seven thousand people as he brag'd to some Oxford scholars'[27]) as a contemporary account given by Richard Baxter suggests:

> Mr. *Coppe and his Followers*, called by some the *Ranters*, by others, the *High-attainers*. This man was a zealous Anabaptist; when I was Preacher to the Garrison of *Coventry*, he was Preacher to the Garrison of *Compton*-house in the same Countrey, and I heard of no opinion that he vented or held, but, the Necessity of Re-baptizing, and Independency, and was a sharp Reproacher of the Ministry... This man continued a most zealous Re-baptizer many years, and re-baptized more than any one man that ever I heard of in the Countrey, witnesse *Warwickshire*, *Oxfordshire*, part of *Worcestershire*,

&c.... He pleads for Community, and against Propriety... And his practice is answerable to his Profesion: For he went up and down teaching this to the poor Professors in the Countrey, and sweareth most hideously in his Conference and Preaching: and cursing, and filthy lascivius practices, not to be named, are his Religion. It may be some will say that he is a mad man: But it is otherwise, as may be known by those that will speak with him, (he is now in *Coventry* Joal, where he was once before upon his re-baptizing[28].

Coppe's initial imprisonment which Baxter refers to here seems to have taken place sometime in 1646[29]. Further evidence that he was a minister of some repute is to be found in issue number sixteen of *Several Proceedings in Parliament* (January 1649 [1650]) which gives the following account of Coppe's second arrest:

> *A Letter from Coventry in Warwickshire.*
> SIR,
>   There is here one *Cops* who was a Minister, (and formerly had a Congregation) apprehended about a Book, which is said he writ, called *THE FLYING ROLL.*
>   Who ever writ it, it is the most blasphemous book that ever I saw or heard of.
>   He was apprehended by a party of Horse, and is to be sent up to the Councell of State; it makes my heart to tremble, to thinke of those fearful blasphemies that are in that book.
>   Truly as for his life, he had formerly good abilities, and did preach well, admirable good Oratory, but afterwards fell to the fearfull sin of being of opinion that he was above Ordinances, and that being a childe of God, he might live as he list, and whatsoever he did he should be saved[30].

  In 1648 Coppe's first published work had appeared. This was a prefatory epistle to a pamphlet entitled *John the Divine's Divinity* by 'J.F.' (whose identity remains unknown), dated the thirteenth of January 1648. This was to be followed in 1649 by Coppe's first important work, a pamphlet entitled *Some Sweet Sips of some Spirituall Wine*, and by a preface to Richard Coppin's *Divine Teachings* which was published in September of the same year[31]. These works were both fiercely critical of formal religion and were to announce some of the themes which were to run through the *Fiery Flying Roll*. Nigel Smith has argued that *Some Sweet Sips* was issued in the Midlands (he points out that there is no copy in the Thomason Collection which was formed in London) but it obviously had some impact as John Osborne, the Presbyterian vicar of Bampton, Oxfordshire, refers to it in his pamphlet *The World to Come, or the Mysterie of the Resurrection* (which also features a conference between Osborne and Richard Coppin)[32].
  It was at the beginning of 1650 with the issue of *A Fiery Flying Roll*, however, that Coppe became more widely known and drew the attention of the authorities in London. The copy of this work in the Thomason Collection is dated the fourth of January 1649 [1650]. As early as the eighth of January it had been ordered by the Council of State, that 'a warrant bee issued to keepe in Custody the person of Coppe, for writing of some blasphemous truths ...'[33] and by the thirteenth it is clear that he was under arrest in

Coventry as the following account demonstrates:

> Coventry Ianuary 13. There is an order come to the Officers here for the removing of Master *Copp the great Anabaptist* from *Warwick* to *Coventry* prison, and there to be continued untill further Order, the reason thereof I understand to be, because he put forth a book intituled, The *fiery flying Roll*, they accordingly brought him to *Coventry* on *Thursday* last, his discourse is altogether unbecoming one that makes a profession of godlinesse as he pretends to doe, swearing and cursing is very common in his usuall discourse hee is very confident that his condition is very good, saying that God cannot damne him. Its reported, that he hath begot many to his judgement that are inhabitants neare Warwick[34].

By the first of February the *Fiery Flying Roll* had attracted the attention of Parliament who issued an order for it to be burnt (see Appendix)[35]. By the third of February an attempt had been made to move Coppe to London but as he was ill and 'desired that he might not take a journey as yet, least it should cost him his life', he was not brought to Newgate until March[36]. Throughout June and July, with Coppe in Newgate, the House of Commons was debating the 'Blasphemy Act' which was eventually passed on the ninth of August (see above)[37]. On the twenty-seventh of September the 'Committee for suppressing licentious and impious Practices, under Pretence of Religion' ordered

> That it be referred to the same Committee, to examine Abiezer Copp, the reputed Author of the Book, called, "The Fiery Flying Roll;" and report the same to the House This-day-sevennight: And this Committee have Power to send for Persons and Witnesses[38].

Of Coppe's examination before this committee two accounts survive, neither very reliable, but worth reproducing if only to demonstrate the kind of attention which Coppe received. The first is an account from a newsbook and the second an extract from one of the sensationalist pamphlets referred to above:

> I had almost forgot to acquaint you with the arrogant and wild deportment of Mr. *Copp* the great Ranter, who made the *Fiery Roll*, who being lately brought before the Commitee of Examinations, refused to be uncovered, and disguised himselfe into a madnesse, flinging Apples and Pears about the roome, wherupon the Commitee returned him to Newgate from whence he came[39].

> Copp is in Newgate... this Copp being lately brought before a Committee to be examined, feigned himself mad, used strange kind of uncouth behaviour, throwing nutshels and other things about the room, and talked to himself when questions were put to him, and others were of the opinion that (as *David* in another case) he meerly acted the part which at length will no way stand him in stead[40].

Other than the fact that a Dr. John Pordage appeared on his behalf at some point, we know nothing of what took place as a result of Coppe's examination except that *A Remonstrance* and *Copp's Return* were both written whilst he was still imprisoned in Newgate[41]. It is evident that Coppe remained in prison until at least the end of June 1651, but by the twenty-third of September he was free and able to preach what was supposed to be a recantation sermon at Burford. John Tickell, who discusses this sermon in *The Bottomless Pit Smoaking in Familisme*, had his doubts as to whether Coppe was repentant at all:

> And as for him, if it may appear by these notes or his own discourse, that he is the same what he was before, only more cunning. 1. To preserve himselfe from barres and bolts, *Newgate a type of Hell*. 2. To deceive others, the very picture *of the Divell*. I say if this appeare (I will not say 'tis so, though you may see my guesse anon) then 1. let the World know what to expect, when the Bottomlesse pit is opened, and the *Divell loosed*. 2. Let the people of God where ever they heare the name of Coppe, look on it as accursed, either stoppe their eares, or pray to God, some way or other to stop his mouth, that he may no more dissable, *blaspheme*[42].

It should be said, however, that Coppe had claimed in the two works he had written in Newgate that he had been unjustly accused and grossly misrepresented, so it is hardly surprising that he should appear 'unrepentant'.

For the next few years after these events Coppe appears still to have been active in London. It is possible that he had connections with a group calling themselves 'My One Flesh' and Lawrence Clarkson [Claxton] mentions him as being in the capital at this time[43]. Whilst a prisoner at Charing-Cross in 1654-55, George Fox received a visit from Coppe as the following account from his 'Journal' relates:

> Among those that came to see me, was one Colonel Packer, with several of his officers; and while they were with me, came in one Cobb, and a great company of Ranters with him. The Ranters began to call for drink and tobacco; but I desired them to forbear it in my room, telling them, if they had such a desire for it, they might go into another room. One of them cried "all is ours;" and another said, "all is well." I replied, "how is all well, while thou art so peevish, and envious, and crabbed?" for I saw he was of a peevish nature. I spoke to their conditions, and they were sensible of it, and looked upon one another, wondering[44].

January 1657 saw the anonymous publication of *Divine Fire-works*, a work which has only recently been attributed to Coppe. It consists of an account of a midnight revelation, related in a style entirely consistent with Coppe's other works[45]. It was at about this time that Coppe changed his name to Dr. Higham and moved to Barnes where he sometimes preached in conventicles. According to Wood (whose hostility to Coppe is obvious even in the account of his death), Coppe

> At length being brought low by certain infirmities which he had contracted in his rambles by drinking and whoring, died there in the month of August in sixteen hundred seventy two[46].

He was buried on the south side of the body of Barnes church on the twenty-third of August 1672. As a postscript to his career, 'A Character of A True Christian' written in verse was published posthumously in 1680.

NOTES

1. Bulstrode Whitelock, *Memorials of the English Affairs* (London: 1682), p.424 (entry dated 2/2/1649).
2. The copy in the Thomason Collection in the British Library is dated (by Thomason) as Jan. 4. 1649. This refers to the regnal year, the start of which was calculated from the date of the death of the previous monarch. Where two dates are given the first refers to the regnal year and the second (in square brackets) to standard reckoning. For further information on regnal years see Chris Cook and John Wroughton, *English Historical Facts 1603-1688* (London: Macmillan, 1980).
3. Norman Cohn, *The Pursuit of the Millenium* (London: Paladin Books, 1978); A.L. Morton, *The World of the Ranters* (London: Lawrence & Wishart, 1970); Christopher Hill, *The World Turned Upside Down* (Harmondsworth: Penguin Books, 1978).
4. Nigel Smith, *A Collection of Ranter Writings* (London: Junction Books, 1983); J.C. Davis, *Fear, Myth and History* (Cambridge: Cambridge University Press, 1986).
5. Abiezer Coppe, *A Fiery Flying Roll* (University of Exeter: The Rota, 1973).
6. See Hill, *op. cit.*
7. Joseph Salmon was the author of *Anti-Christ in Man* (1647), *A rout, a rout* (1649) and *Heights in Depths and Depths in Heights* (1651). Like Coppe, he was arrested and imprisoned at Coventry (see note 9. below). Lawrence Clarkson is perhaps best known for the autobiographical account of his religious career, *The Lost Sheep Found* (1660). He was brought up a Puritan but underwent a series of conversions including, supposedly, one to 'Ranterism' and died a Mugarletonian. Jacob Bauthumley, while still in the Army, published *The Light and Dark Sides of God* (1650) which was condemned as blasphemous and for which he was sentenced to be bored through the tongue. These three, together with Coppe, are usually considered to be the major 'Ranters'. Representative works by all of them can be found in Smith, *op. cit.*.
8. Davis, *op. cit.*; While Coppe was imprisoned at Coventry, Salmon was also arrested and imprisoned. In a letter to Thomas Webbe (reprinted in Edward Stokes, *The Wiltshire Rant* [London: 1652], p.13) Salmon writes: 'Cop, *my, thy own hart is gone to* London'. There is also evidence of a connection between Andrew Wyke, who had gone to Coventry to visit Coppe, and Salmon: see *Report on the Manuscripts of F.W. Leybourne-Popham* (Norwich: H.M.S.O., 1899), p.57, which contains a letter of Robert Beake, gaoler to both Coppe and Salmon; and also *A Perfect Diurnall*, No.14 11-18/3/1649 [1650].
9. David Masson, *The Life of Milton* (London: Macmillan, 1877), Vol.V, p.18.
10. *The Routing of the Ranters* (London: 1650), p.3. See also *The Ranters Ranting* (London: 1650) and *The Arraignment and Tryall With A Declaration of the Ranters* (London: 1650).
11. Davis, *op. cit.*, p.87.
12. *Ibid.*, p.91.
13. For Joachim of Fiore see Cohn, *op. cit.*.
14. A.L. Morton, 'The Everlasting Gospel' in Morton, *The Matter of Britain* (London: Lawrence & Wishart, 1966), p.101.
15. Davis, *op. cit.*, p.53.
16. *Ibid.*, p.54.
17. See *A Remonstrance* below.

18. *An Act against several Atheistical, Blasphemous and Execrable Opinions, derogatory to the honor of God, and destructive to humane Society*, (9 August, 1650), reprinted in C.H. Firth & R.S. Rait, *Acts and Ordinances of the Interregnum, 1642-1660* (London: H.M.S.O., 1911), Vol. II, pp.409-12.
19. Davis, *op. cit.*, p.55.
20. Hill, *op. cit.*, p.212.
21. Davis, *op. cit.*, p.57.
22. Hill, *op. cit.*, p.210.
23. See Morton, 'The Everlasting Gospel'; J.E.V. Crofts, *Wordsworth and the Seventeenth Century* (London: Humphrey Milford, 1940).
24. Davis, *op. cit.*, p.48.
25. Anthony Wood, *Athenæ Oxonienses*, ed. Philip Bliss (London: 1815), pp.959-62.
26. *Ibid.*, pp.959-60.
27. *Ibid.*, *loc. cit.*.
28. Richard Baxter, *Plain Scripture Proof of Infants Church-membership and Baptism* (London: 1651), p.148.
29. See Thomas Crosby, *History of the English Baptists* (London: 1738), p.224.
30. *Several Proceedings in Parliament* No. 16, 11/1/1649 [1650], p.213.
31. All three of these works are reprinted in Smith, *op. cit.*.
32. *Ibid.*, p.12; John Osborne, *The World to Come* (London: 1651), Sig. A2.
33. Public Records Office, SP25 63, p.485, No.5.
34. *A Perfect Diurnall* No. 6, 14-21/1/1649 [1650], p.42.
35. See also *Journals of the House of Commons* Vol. VI, p.354; *Mercurius Pragmaticus*, Part 2, No. 41, 5-12/2/1649 [1650]; *Several Procedings in Parliament* No. 19, 31/1/1649 [1650]; Whitelock, *op. cit.*, p.424; *A Perfect Diurnall* No.8, 28/1/1649 [1650] - 4/2/1649 [1650], p.72.
36. *A Perfect Diurnall* No. 9, 4-11/2/1649 [1650], p.76. See also Public Records Office, SP25 63, p.588, No.5; *A Perfect Diurnall* No. 15, 18-25/3/1649 [1650], p.141.
37. For the preceeding debate see *Journals of the House of Commons* Vol. VI, pp. 427, 430, 437, 440, 443-44, 453.
38. *Journals of the House of Commons* Vol. VI, p.475.
39. *The Weekly Intelligencer of the Common-Wealth* 1-8/10/1649 [1650], p.10.
40. *The Routing of the Ranters*, p.2.
41. See Christopher Fowler, *Dæmonium Meridianum* (London: 1655), p.60. and Wood, *op. cit.*, p.1099.
42. John Tickell, *The Bottomless Pit Smoaking in Familisme* (Oxford: 1651), p.35.
43. See Smith, *op. cit.*, p.13 and Lawrence Claxton, *The Lost Sheep Found*, (London: 1660), pp.25-6.
44. George Fox, *Journal Of George Fox* (London: 1891), 8th ed., p.211.
45. Owen C. Watkins, *The Puritan Experience* (London: Routledge & Kegan Paul, 1972), p.147.
46. Wood, *op. cit.*, pp.961-2.

A NOTE ON THE TEXT:

The works reproduced in this edition follow as faithfully as possible the original publications, currently in the possession of the British Library. A few alterations have been made in the case of obvious typographical errors, otherwise Coppe's spelling and punctuation have been preserved throughout. The layout of the original pamphlets and broadsheets has also been followed, though this has been rationalised to fit the format of the present edition. In all instances our aim has been to make the texts as readable and as accurate as possible.

With the exception of *A Character of a True Christian* the texts form part of the Thomason Collection in the British Library. The catalogue references and Thomason's date of acquisition are as follows: *A Fiery Flying Roll*, E.587 (13, 14), January 4, 1650; *Die Veneris, I Februarii, 1649*, 669.f.15 (10), February 1, 1650; *A Remonstrance of the sincere and zealous Protestation of Abiezer Coppe*, E.621 (5), January 3, 1651; *Copp's Return to the wayes of Truth*, E.637 (14), July 11, 1651; *Divine Fire-Works*, 669.f.20 (45), January 21, 1657.

The catalogue reference for *A Character of a True Christian* (1680) is Lutt. II. 35.

Acknowledgements: I would like to thank the staff of the British Library for their assistance. I would also like to thank Ed Baxter for his invaluable help and advice in preparing this volume.

A Fiery Flying Roll:

A
Word from the Lord to all the Great Ones
of the Earth, whom this may concerne: Being the
last WARNING PIECE at the dreadfull day of
JUDGEMENT.
For now the LORD is come

to $\left\{\begin{array}{l} 1\ \textit{Informe} \\ 2\ \textit{Advise and warne} \\ 3\ \textit{Charge} \\ 4\ \textit{Judge and sentence} \end{array}\right\}$ the Great Ones.

As also most
compassionately informing, and most lovingly and pathetically
advising and warning *London*.

With a terrible Word, and fatall Blow from the LORD,
upon the Gathered CHURCHES.

And all by his Most Excellent MAJESTY, dwelling
in, and shining through
AUXILIUM PATRIS, בך alias, *Coppe*.
With another FLYING ROLL ensuing (to all the Inhabitants of the
Earth.) The Contents of both following.

Isa. 23.9, *The Lord of Hosts (is) staining the pride of all glory, and bringing into*
contempt all the honourable (persons and things) of the Earth.
O London, London, how would I gather thee, as a hen gathereth her chickens under
her wings, &c.
Know thou (in this day) the things that belong to thy Peace —— I know the
blasphemy of them which say they are Jewes, and are not, but are the
Synagogue of Satan, Rev. 2.9.

Imprinted at *London*, in the beginning of that notable day, wherein
the secrets of all hearts are laid open; and wherein the worst and
foulest of villanies, are discovered, under the best and fairest
outsides. 1649.

THE PREFACE

An inlet into the Land of Promise, the new
Hierusalem, and a gate into the ensuing Discourse,
worthy of serious consideration.

MY Deare One.
All or None.
Every one under the Sunne.
Mine own.
My most Excellent Majesty (in me) hath strangely and variously transformed this forme.

And behold, by mine owne Almightinesse (In me) I have been changed in a moment, in the twinkling of an eye, at the sound of the Trump.

And now the Lord is descended from Heaven, with a shout, with the voyce of the Arch-angell, and with the Trump of God.

And the sea, the earth, yea all things are now giving up their dead. And all things that ever were, are, or shall be visible —— are the Grave wherein the King of Glory (the eternall, invisible Almightinesse, hath lain as it were) dead and buried.

But behold, behold, he is now risen with a witnesse, to save *Zion* with vengeance, or to confound and plague all things into himself; who by his mighty Angell is proclaiming (with a loud voyce) That Sin and Transgression is finished and ended; and everlasting righteousnesse brought in; and the everlasting Gospell preaching; Which everlasting Gospell is brought in with most terrible earth-quakes, and heaven-quakes, and with signes and wonders following. *Amen.*

And it hath pleased my most Excellent Majesty, (who is universall love, and whose service is perfect freedome) to set this forme (the Writer of this Roll) as no small signe and wonder in fleshly *Israel*; as you may partly see in the ensuing Discourse.

And now (my deare ones!) every one under the Sun, I will onely point at the gate; thorow which I was led into that new City, new *Hierusalem*, and to the Spirits of just men, made perfect, and to God the Judge of all.

First, all my strength, my forces were utterly routed, my

house I dwelt in fired; my father and mother forsook me, the wife of my bosome loathed me, mine old name was rotted, perished; and I was utterly plagued, consumed, damned, rammed, and sunke into nothing, into the bowels of the still Eternity (my mothers wombe) out of which I came naked, and whetherto I returned again naked. And lying a while there, rapt up in silence, at length (the body or outward forme being awake all this while) I heard with my outward eare (to my apprehension) a most terrible thunder-clap, and after that a second. And upon the second thunder-clap, which was exceeding terrible, I saw a great body of light, like the light of the Sun, and red as fire, in the forme of a drum (as it were) whereupon with exceeding trembling and amazement on the flesh, and with joy unspeakable in the spirit, I clapt my hands, and cryed out, *Amen, Halelujah, Halelujah, Amen. A*nd so lay trembling, sweating, and smoaking (for the space of half an houre) at length with a loud voyce (I inwardly) cryed out, Lord, what wilt thou do with me; my most excellent majesty and eternal glory (in me) answered & sayd, Fear not, I will take thee up into mine everlasting Kingdom. But thou shalt (first) drink a bitter cup, a bitter cup, a bitter cup; whereupon (being filled with exceeding amazement) I was throwne into the belly of hell (and take what you can of it in these expressions, though the matter is beyond expression) I was among all the Devils in hell, even in their most hideous hew.

And under all this terrour, and amazement, there was a little spark of transcendent, transplendent, unspeakable glory, which survived, and sustained it self, triumphing, exulting, and exalting it self above all the Fiends. And, confounding the very blacknesse of darknesse (you must take it in these tearmes, for it is infinitely beyond expression.) Upon this the life was taken out of the body (for a season) and it was thus resembled, as if a man with a great brush dipt in whiting, should with one stroke wipe out, or sweep off a picture upon a wall, &c. after a while, breath and life was returned into the form againe; whereupon I saw various streames of light (in the night) which appeared to the outward eye; and immediately I saw three hearts (or three appearances) in the form of hearts, of exceeding brightnesse; and immediately an innumerable company of hearts, filling each corner of the room where I was. And methoughts there was variety and distinction, as if there had been severall hearts, and yet most strangely and unexpressibly complicated or folded up in unity. I clearly saw distinction, diversity, variety, and as clearly saw all

A.C.—B

swallowed up into unity. And it hath been my song many times since, within and without, unity, universality, universality, unity, Eternall Majesty, &c. And at this vision, a most strong, glorious voyce uttered these words, *The spirits of just men made perfect.* the spirits &c, with whom I had as absolut, cleare, full communion, and in a two fold more familiar way, then ever I had outwardly with my dearest friends, and nearest relations. The visions and revelations of God, and the strong hand of eternall invisible almightinesse, was stretched out upon me, within me, for the space of foure dayes and nights, without intermission. The time would faile if I would tell you all, but it is not the good will and pleasure of my most excellent Majesty in me, to declare any more (as yet) then thus much further: That amongst those various voyces that were then uttered within, these were some, *Blood, blood, Where, where? upon the hypocriticall holy heart, &c.* Another thus, *Vengeance, vengeance, vengeance, Plagues, plagues, upon the Inhabitants of the earth; Fire, fire, fire, Sword, sword, &c. upon all that bow not down to eternall Majesty, universall love; I'le recover, recover, my wooll, my flax, my money. Declare, declare, feare thou not the faces of any; I am (in thee) a munition of Rocks, &c.*

Go up to *London*,* to *London*, that great City, write, write, write. And behold I writ, and lo a hand was sent to me, and a roll of a book was therein, which this fleshly hand would have put wings to, before the time. Whereupon it was snatcht out of my hand, & the Roll thrust into my mouth; and I eat it up, and filled my bowels with it, (*Eze.* 2.8. &c. cha. 3.1,2,3.) where it was as bitter as worm-wood; and it lay broiling, and burning in my stomack, till I brought it forth in this forme.

And now I send it flying to thee, with my heart, And all,

Per AUXILIUM PATRIS בך

18

THE CONTENTS.

CHAP.1. **S**Everall Strange, yet true and seasonable informations to the great ones, as also an apologeticall hint of the Authors principle, &c.

CHAP.2. Severall new, strange, yet seasonable and good advice, and wholsome admonitions, and the last warning to the great ones, as from the Lord.

CHAP.3. Severall dismall, dolefull cryes, & out-cries, which pierce the eares and heart of his excellent Majesty, & how the King of Kings, the King of heaven charges the great ones of the earth.

CHAP.4. How the Judge of heaven and earth, who judgeth righteous judgment, passeth sentence against all those great ones, who like sturdy Oakes & tall Cedars wil not bow, and how hee intends to breake them, and blow them up by the roots.

CHAP.5. A most compassionate information, and a most loving & patheticall warning and advice to London.

CHAP.6. A terrible word and fatall blow from the Lord upon the gathered Churches, who pretend most for God, yet defie the Almighty more then the vilest.

The second Flying Roll.

CHAP.1. The Authors commission to write. A terrible woe denounced against those that slight the roll. The Lords claim to all things; Together with a hint of a two-fold recovery, where-through the most hypocriticall heart shall be ripped up, &c.

CHAP.2. How the Lord will recover his outward things (things of this life) as money, corn, wool, flax, &c. and for whom: And how they shal be plagued that detaine them as their owne. Wherein also are some mistical hints concerning St. Michaels day, and the Lords day following it this yeare; as also of the dominicall letter D, &c.

CHAP.3. A strange, yet most true storie, under which is couched that lion,

whose roaring shall make all the beasts of the field to tremble, and all the kingdomes of the world quake.

Wherein also (in part) the subtilty of the welfavour'd harlot is discovered, and her flesh burnt with that fire which shall burn down all Churches, except that of the first borne, &c.

CHAP.4. That the Author hath been set as a sign and wonder, &c. as well as most of the Prophets formerly; as also what strange posturs that divine Majestie (that dwels in his forme) hath set the forme in: with the most strange and various effects thereof upon the Spectators. His communion with the spirits of Just men made perfect, and with God the Judg of all hinted at.

CHAP.5. *The Authors strange and lofty carriage towards great ones, & his most lowly carriage towards beggars, rogues, prisoners, gypsies, &c. Together with a large Declaration what glory shall arise up from under all these ashes. The most strange & most secret and terrible, yet most glorious designe of God, in choosing base things, to confound things that are: And, how, A most terrible viall poured out upon the well-favoured harlot; and how the Lord is bringing into contempt not only honourable persons (with a vengeance) but all honourable holy things also.*

Wholsome advice, with a terrible threat to the Formalists: And how BASE things have confounded base things: And how base things have been a fiery chariot to mount the Author up into divine glory and unspeakable Majestie: And how his wife is, & his life is in that beauty, which maketh visible beauty seem meere deformity.

CHAP.6. *Great ones must bow to the poorest peasants, or else they shall rue for it; No material sword or humane power (whatsoever) but the pure spirit of universall love, who is the eternall God, can breake the necke of tyranny, oppression, and abhominable pride and cruell murther, &c. A catalogue of severall Judgments recited, as so many warning-pieces to appropriators, impropriators, and anti-free communicants.*

CHAP.7. *A further discovery of the subtilty of the well favoured harlot, with a parley between her and the spirit. As also the horrid villany that lies hid under her smooth words, and sweet tongue (in pleading against the letter and history, and for the spirit and mistery, and all for her own ends) detected. Also upon what account the spirit is put, and upon what account the letter, &c. And what the true communion, and what the true breaking of bread is.*

CHAP.8. *The wel-favoured harlots cloaths stript off, her nakednesse discovered, her nose slit. Her hunting after the young man void of understanding, from corner to corner, from religion to religion: And the spirit pursuing, overtaking, and destroying her, &c.*

With a terrible thunder-clap i'th close.

A word from the Lord to all the Great Ones of the Earth (whom this may concerne) being the last Warning Piece, &c.

1 *The word of the Lord came expresly to me, saying, Sonne of man write a Roule, and these words, from my mouth, to the Great ones, saying, thus saith the Lord:*

Slight not this Roule, neither laugh at it, least I slight you, and cause all men to slight and scorne you; least I destroy you, and laugh at your destruction, &c.

2 *This is, (and with a witnesse, some of you shall finde it, to be) an edg'd toole; and there's no jesting with it, or laughing at it.*

It's a sharp sword, sharpned, and also fourbished ——

No sleepy Dormouse shall dare to creep up the edge of it.

Thus saith the Lord, You shall finde with a witnesse, that I am now comming

to $\left\{\begin{array}{l} 1\ Informe \\ 2\ Advise\ and\ warne \\ 3\ Charge \\ 4\ Judge\ and\ sentence \end{array}\right\}$ *you, O ye great ones.*

CHAP. 1.

Containing severall strange, yet true and seasonable Informations, to the great ones. As also an apologeticall hint, of the Authors Principle, standing in the front. ——

1. Thus saith the Lord, *I inform you, that I overturn, overturn, overturn.* And as the Bishops, *Charles,* and the Lords, have had their turn, overturn, so your turn shall be next (ye surviving great ones) by what Name or Title soever dignified or distinguished) who ever you are, that

oppose me, the Eternall God, who am UNIVERSALL Love, and whose service is perfect freedome, and pure Libertinisme.

*An Apologeticall hint concerning the Authors Principle, the result—— is negative; hee speaks little in the affirmative because not one in a hundred, yea even of his former acquaintance, now know him, neither must they yet.

2* But afore I proceed any further, be it known to you, That although that excellent Majesty, which dwels in the Writer of this Roule, hath reconciled ALL THINGS to himselfe, yet this hand (which now writes) never drew sword, or shed one drop of any mans blood. [I am free from the blood of all men] though (I say) all things are reconciled to me, the eternall God (IN HIM) yet sword levelling, or digging-levelling, are neither of them his principle.

Both are as farre from his principle, as the East is from the West, or the Heavens from the Earth (though, I say, reconciled to both, as to all things else) and though he hath more justice, righteousnesse, truth, and sincerity, shining in those low dung-hils, (as they are esteemed) then in the Sunne, Moone, and all the Stars.

3 I come not forth (in him) either with materiall sword, or Mattock, but now (in this my day ——) I make him my Sword-bearer, to brandish the Sword of the Spirit, as he hath done severall dayes and nights together, thorow the streets of the great City.

4 And now thus saith the Lord:

Though you can as little endure the word LEVELLING, as could the late slaine or dead *Charles* (your forerunner, who is gone before you ——) and had as live heare the Devill named, as heare of the Levellers (Men-Levellers) which is, and who (indeed) are but shadows of most terrible, yet great and glorious good things to come.

5 Behold, behold, behold, I the eternall God, the Lord of Hosts, who am that mighty Leveller, am comming (yea even at the doores) to Levell in good earnest, to Levell to some purpose, to Levell with a witnesse, to Levell the Hills with the Valleyes, and to lay the Mountaines low.

6 High Mountaines! lofty Cedars! its high time for you to enter into the Rocks, and to hide you in the dust, for feare of the Lord, and for the glory of his Majesty. For the lofty looks of man shall be humbled, and the haughtinesse of men shall be bowed downe, and the Lord ALONE shall be exalted in that day; For the day of the Lord of Hoasts, shall be upon every one that is proud, and lofty, and upon every one that is lifted up, and he shall be brought low. And upon all the Cedars of *Lebanon*, that are high and lifted up, and upon all the Oaks of *Bashan*; and upon all the high Mountaines; and upon all the Hils that are lifted up, and upon every high Tower; and upon every fenced Wall; and upon all the Ships of *Tarshish*, and upon all pleasant

Pictures.

And the LOFTINESSE of man shall be bowed down, and the haughtinesse of men shall be laid low. And the Lord ALONE shall be exalted in that day, and the Idols he shall utterly abolish.

And they shall go into the the holes of the Rocks, and into the Caves of the Earth, for feare of the Lord, and for the glory of his Majesty, when he ariseth to shake terribly the earth.

In that day a man shall cast his Idols of Silver, and Idols of Gold —— to the bats, and to the Moles. To go into the Clefts of the Rocks and into the tops of the ragged Rocks, for feare of the Lord, and for the glory of his Majesty. For the Lord is now RISEN to shake terribly the Earth, *Isa.* 2.10. to of the Chapter.

7 Hills! Mountains! Cedars! Mighty men! Your breath is in your nostrils.

Those that have admired, adored, idolized, magnified, set you up, fought for you, ventured goods, and good name; limbe and life for you, shall cease from you.

You shall not (at all) be accounted of (not one of you) ye sturdy Oake) who bowe not downe before eternall Majesty: Universall Love, whose service is perfect freedome, and who hath put down the mighty (remember, remember your fore-runner) and who is putting down the mighty from their feats; and exalting them of low degree.

8 Oh let not, (for your owne sakes) let not the mother of Harlots in you, who is very subtle of heart.

Nor the Beast (without you) what do you call 'em? The Ministers, fat parsons, Vicars, Lecturers, &c. who (for their owne base ends, to maintaine their pride, and pompe, and to fill their owne paunches, and purses) have been the chiefe instruments of all those horrid abominations, hellish, cruell, devillish persecutions, in this Nation which cry for vengeance. For your owne sakes (I say) let neither the one, nor the other bewitch you, or charme your cares, to heare them say, these things shall not befall you, these Scriptures shall not be fulfilled upon you, but upon the Pope, Turke, and Heathen Princes, &c.

9 Or if any of them should (through subtilty for their owne base ends) creep into the Mystery of that fore-mentioned* Scripture.   *Isay 2:

And tell you, Those words are to be taken in the Mystery only; and they onely point out a spirituall, inward levelling (once more, for your owne sakes, I say) believe them not.

10 'Tis true, the History, or Letter, (I speake comparatively) is but as it were haire-cloth; the Mystery is fine Flax. My

flax, saith the Lord, and the Thief and the Robber will steale from me my flax, to cover his nakednesse, that his filthinesse may not appeare.

But behold, I am (now) recovering my flax out of his hand, and discovering his lewdnesse — *verbum sat* —

11 'Tis true, the Mystery is my joy, my delight, my life.

And the Prime levelling, is laying low the Mountaines, and levelling the Hils in man.

But this is not all.

For lo I come (saith the Lord) with a vengeance, to levell also your Honour, Riches, &c. to staine the pride of all your glory, and to bring into contempt all the Honourable (both persons and things) upon the earth, Isa. 23,9.

12 For this Honour, Nobility, Gentility, Propriety, Superfluity, &c. hath (without contradiction) been the Father of hellish horrid pride, arrogance, haughtinesse, loftinesse, murder, malice, of all manner of wickednesse and impiety; yea the cause of all the blood that ever hath been shed, from the blood of righteous *Abell*, to the blood of the last Levellers that were shot to death. *And now (as I live saith the Lord) I am come to make inquisition for blood; for murder and pride, &c.*

13 I see the root of it all. *The Axe is laid to the root of the Tree* (by Eternall God, *My Self*, saith the Lord) *I will hew it down.* And as I live, I will plague your Honour, Pompe, Greatnesse, Superfluity, and confound it into parity, equality, community; that the neck of horrid pride, murder, malice, and tyranny, &c. may be chopt off at one blow. And that my selfe, the Eternall God, who am Universall Love, may fill the Earth with universall love, universall peace, and perfect freedome; which can never be by humane sword or strength accomplished.

14 Wherefore bow downe, bow downe, you sturdy Oakes, and tall Cedars; bow, or by my self Ile break you.

Ile cause some of you (on whom I have compassion) to bow &c. and will terribly plague the rest.

My little finger shall be heavier on them, then my whole loynes were on *Pharoah* of old.

15 And maugre the subtilty, and sedulity, the craft and cruelty of hell, and earth: this Levelling shall up.

Not by sword; we (holily) scorne to fight for any thing; we had as live be dead drunk every day of the weeke, and lye with whores i'th the market place, and account these as good actions as taking the poore abused, enslaved ploughmans money from him (who is almost every where undone, and squeezed to death; and not so much as that plaguy, unsupportable, hellish burden, and oppression, of

Tythes taken off his shoulders, notwithstanding all his honesty, fidelity, Taxes, Freequarter, petitioning &c. for the same,) we had rather starve, I say, then take away his money from him, for killing of men.

Nay, if we might have Captains pay, and a good fat Parsonage or two besides, we would scorne to be swordsmen, or fight with those (mostly) carnall weapons, for any thing, or against any one, or for our livings.

16 No, no, wee'l live in despite of our foes; and this levelling (to thy torment, O mighty man) shall up, not by sword, not by might, &c. but by my Spirit, saith the Lord.

For I am risen, for I am risen, for I am risen, to shake terribly the earth, and not the earth onely, but the heavens also, &c.

But here I shall cease informing you.

You may for your further information (if you please) reade my Roule to all the rich Inhabitants of the earth.

Reade it if you be wise, I shall now advice you.

CHAP. II.

Containing severall new, strange, yet seasonable Admonitions, and good advice; as the last warning to the Great Ones of the Earth. from the Lord.

1 THus saith the Lord: Be* wise now therefore, O ye Rulers, &c. Be instructed, &c. Kisse the Sunne, &c.

Yea, kisse Beggers, Prisoners, warme them, feed them, cloathe them, money them, relieve them, release them, take them into your houses, don't serve them as dogs, without doore. &c.

Owne them, they are flesh of your flesh, your owne brethren, your owne Sisters, every whit as good (and if I should stand in competition with you) in some degrees better then your selves.

2 Once more, I say, own them; they are your self, make them one with you, or else go howling into hell; howle for the miseries that are comming upon you, howle.

The very shadow of levelling, sword-levelling, man-levelling, frighted you, (and who, like your selves, can blame you, because it shook your Kingdome?) but now the substantiality of levelling is coming.

The Eternall God, the mighty Leveller is comming, yea come, even at the doore; and what will you do in that day.

Repent, repent, repent, Bow down, bow down, bow, or howle, resigne, or be damned; Bow downe, bow downe, you sturdy Oakes, and Cedars, bow downe.

Veile too, and kisse the meaner shrubs. Bow, or else (by my self saith the Lord) Ile breake you in pieces (some of you) others I will teare up by the roots; I will suddenly deale with you all, some in one way; some in another. Wherefore

Each Begger that you meet
Fall down before him, kisse him in the street.

Once more, he is thy brother, thy fellow, flesh of thy flesh.

Turne not away thine eyes from thine owne FLESH, least I pull out thine eyes and throw thee headlong into hell.

3 Mine eares are filled brim full with cryes of poore prisoners, Newgate, Ludgate cryes (of late) are seldome out of mine eares. Those dolefull cryes, Bread, bread, bread for the Lords sake, pierce mine eares, and heart, I can no longer forbeare.

Werefore high you apace to all prisons in the Kingdome,

2 Admonition to great ones.

4 Bow before those poore, nasty, lousie, ragged wretches, say to them, your humble servants, Sirs, (without a complement) we let you go free, and serve you, &c.

Do this (or as I live saith the Lord) thine eyes (at least) shall be boared out, and thou carried captive into a strange Land.

3 Admonition to great ones

5 Give over, give over, thy odious, nasty, abominable fasting, for strife and debate, and to smite with the fist of wickednesse. And instead thereof, loose the bands of wickednesse, undo the heavy burdens, let the oppressed go free, and breake every yoake. Deale thy bread to the hungry, and bring the poore that are cast out (both of houses and Synagogues) to thy house. Cover the naked: Hide not thy self from thine own flesh, from a creeple, a rogue, a begger, he's thine owne flesh. From a Whore-monger, a thief, &c. he's flesh of thy flesh, and his theft, and whoredome is flesh of thy flesh also, thine owne flesh. Thou maist have ten, times more of each within thee, then he that acts outwardly in either, Remember, turn not away thine eyes from thine OWN FLESH.

4 Admonition to great ones

6 Give over, give over thy midnight mischief.

Let branding with the letter *B.* alone.

Be no longer so horridly, hellishly, impudently, arrogant-ly, wicked, as to judge what is sinne, what not, what evill, and what not, what blasphemy, and what not.

For thou and all thy reverend Divines, so called (who Divine for Tythes, hire, and money, and serve the Lord Jesus Christ for their owne bellyes) are ignorant of this one thing.

7 That sinne and transgression is finisht, its a meere riddle, that they, with all their humane learning can never reade.

Neither can they understand what pure honour is wrapt up in the Kings Motto, *Honi Soit qui Mal. y. Pense.* Evill to him that evill thinks.

Some there are (who are accounted the off scouring of all things) who are Noble Knights of the Garter. Since which —— they could see no evill, thinke no evill, doe no evill, know no evill.

ALL is Religion that they speak, and honour that they do.

But all you that eat of the Tree of Knowledge of Good and Evill, and have not your Evill eye Pickt out, you call Good Evill, and Evill Good; Light Darknesse, and Darknesse Light; Truth Blasphemy, and Blasphemy Truth.

And you are at this time of your Father the Devill, and of your brother the Pharisee, who still say of Christ (who is now alive) say we not well that he hath a Devill.

9 Take heed, take heed, take heed.

Filthy blinde Sodomites called Angels men, they seeing no further then the formes of men.

10 There are Angels (now) come downe from Heaven, in the shapes and formes of men, who are full of the vengeance of the Lord; and are to poure out the plagues of God upon the Earth, and to torment the Inhabitants thereof.

Some of these Angels I have been acquainted withall.

And I have looked upon them as Devils, accounting them Devils incarnate, and have run from place to place, to hide my self from them, shunning their company; and have been utterly ashamed when I have been seen with them.

But for my labour; I have been plagued and tormented beyond expression. So that now I had rather behold one of these Angels *pouring out the plagues of God, cursing; and teaching others to curse bitterly.

*Rev. 15, Judges 5, Revel. 10, Neh. 13.25,

And had rather heare a mighty Angell (in man) swearing a full-mouthed Oath; and see the spirit of *Nehemiah* (in any form of man, or woman) running upon an uncleane Jew (a pretended Saint) and tearing the haire of his head like a mad man, cursing, and making others fall a swearing, then heare a zealous Presbyterian, Independent, or* spirituall Notionist, pray, preach, or exercise.

*This will come in request with you next; you may remember that Independency, which is now so hug'd, was counted blasphemy, and banishment was too good for it.

11 Well! To the pure all things are pure. God hath so cleared cursing, swearing, in some, that that which goes for swearing and cursing in them, is more glorious then praying and preaching in others.

And what God hath cleansed, call thou not uncleane.

27

And if *Peter* prove a great transgressor of the Law, by doing that which was as odious as killing a man; if he at length (though he be loath at first) eat that which was common and unclean &c. (I give but a hint) blame him not, much lesse lift up a finger against, or plant a hellish Ordinance —— against him, least thou be plagued, and damned too, for thy zeale, blinde Religion, and fleshly holinesse, which now stinks above ground, though formerly it had a good favour.

12 But O thou holy, zealous, devout, righteous, religious one (whoever thou art) that seest evill, or any thing uncleane; do thou sweare, if thou darest, if it be but (I'faith) I'le throw thee to Hell for it (saith the Lord) and laugh at thy destruction.

While Angels (in the forme of men) shall sweare, Heart, Blood, Wounds, and by the Eternall God, &c. in profound purity, and in high Honour, and Majesty.

13 Well! one hint more; there's swearing ignorantly, i'th darke, vainely, and there's swearing i'th light, gloriously.

Well! man of the earth! Lord *Esau*! what hast thou to do with those who sweare upon the former account?

Vengeance is mine, Judgement, Hell, Wrath, &c. all is mine (saith the Lord) dare not thou to set thy foot so impudently and arrogantly upon one step of my Throne: I am Judge my self —— Be wise, give over, have done ——

14 And as for the latter sort of swearing, thou knowest it not when thou hearest it. It's no new thing for thee to call Christ Beel-zebub, and Beel-zebub Christ; to call a holy Angell a Devill, and a Devill an Angell.

15 I charge thee (in the name of Eternall God) meddle not with either, let the Tares alone, least thou pull up the Wheat also, woe be to thee if thou dost. Let both alone (I say) least thou shouldest happen of a holy swearing Angell, and take a Lion by the paw to thine owne destruction.

Never was there such a time since the world stood, as now is.

Thou knowest not the strange appearances of the Lord, now a daies. Take heed, know thou hast been warned.

5 Admonition to great ones. 16 And whatever thou dost, dip not thy little finger in blood any more, thou art up to the elbowes already: Much sope, yea much nitre cannot cleanse thee, &c.

Much more have I to say to thee (saith the Lord) but I will do it secretly; and dart a quiver full of arrowes into thy heart; and I will now charge thee.

CHAP. III.

Containing severall dismall, dolefull cryes, and outcries. which pierce the eares and heart of his Excellent Majesty, the King of Kings. And how the King of Heaven chargeth the Great Ones of the Earth.

1 THus saith the Lord, Be silent, O all flesh, before the Lord; be silent; O lofty, haughty, great ones of the Earth.

There are so many Bils of Indictment preferred against thee, that both heaven and earth blush thereat.

How long shall I heare the sighs and groanes, and see the teares of poore widowes; and heare curses in every corner; and all sorts of people crying out oppression, oppression, tyranny, tyranny, the worst of tyranny, unheard of, unnaturall tyranny.

—— O my back, my shoulders. O Tythes, Excize, Taxes, Pollings, &c. O Lord! O Lord God Almighty!

What, a little finger heavier then former loynes?

What have I engaged my goods, my life, &c. forsooke my dearest relations, and all for liberty and true freedome, for freedome from oppression, and more laid on my back, &c.

2 Mine eares are filled brim full with confused noise, cries, and outcries; O the innumerable complaints and groanes that pierce my heart (thorow and thorow) O astonishing complaints.

Was ever the like ingratitude heard of since the world stood? what! best friends, surest friends, slighted, scorned, and that which cometh from them (in the basest manner) contemned, and some rewarded with prisons, some with death?

O the abominable perfidiousnesse, falseheartednesse; self-seeking, self-inriching, and Kingdome-depopulating, and devastating, &c.

These, and divers of the same nature, are the cries of *England*.

And can I any longer forbeare?

I have heard, I have heard, the groaning of my people. And now I come to deliver them, saith the Lord.

Woe be to *Pharaoh* King of *Egypt*.

You Great Ones that are not tackt nor tainted, you may laugh and sing, whom this hitteth it hitteth. And it shall hit home.

And this which followeth, all whom it concerneth, by what name or title soever dignified or distinguished.

3 You mostly hate those (called Levellers) who (for ought

you know) acted as they did, out of the sincerity, simplicity, and fidelity of their hearts; fearing least they should come under the notion of Covenant breakers, if they did not so act.

Which if so, then were they most barbarously, unnaturally, hellishly murdered; and they died Martyrs for God and their Countrey.

And their blood cries vengeance, vengeance, in mine eares, saith the Lord.

*Once more know, that Sword-leveling is not my principle; I onely pronounce the righteous judgements of the Lord upon Earth, as I durst.

4 Well! let it be how it will; these* Levellers (so called) you mostly hated, though in outward declarations you owned their Tenents as your own Principle.

So you mostly hate me (saith the Lord) though in outward declarations you professe me, and seem to owne me, more then a thousand whom you despise, and account worse than your selves, who are neerer the Kingdome of Heaven then your selve.

You have killed Levellers (so called) you also (with wicked hands) have slain me the Lord of life, who am now risen, and risen indeed, (and you shall know, and feele it with a witnesse) to Levell you in good earnest. And to lay low all high hils, and every mountaine that is high, and lifted up, &c.

5 Well! once more, read *Jam*.5, 1.to 7 —— Ye have killed the just —— Ye have killed, ye have killed, ye have killed the just.

The blood cryeth in mine eares, Vengeance, vengeance, vengeance, vengeance is mine, I will recompence.

Well! what will you do with *Bray*, and the poore prisoners elsewhere? You know not what you do.

You little know what will become of you.

One of you had best remember your dream about your Fathers Moule ——

6 Neither do I forget the one hundred spent in superfluous dishes (at your late great *London* Feast, for I know what ——) when hundreds of poore wretches dyed with hunger.

I have heard a sound in mine eares, that no lesse then a hundred died in one week, pined, and starved with hunger.

Howle you great ones, for all the feast daies dole, &c. heare your doome.

CHAP. IV.

How the Judge of Heaven and Earth, who judgeth righteous judgement, passeth sentence against all those Great Ones, who (like Oakes and tall Cedars) will not bow. And how he intends to blow them up by the roots.

1 T Hus saith the Lord: All you tall Cedars, and sturdy
Oakes, who bow not down, who bow not down —
This sentence is gone out of my mouth against you,
MENE, MENE, TEKEL.
Thou art weighed in the ballances, and art found wanting.
God hath numbred thy Kingdome, and finished it.

And thou, and all that joyne with thee, or are (in the least degree) accessary to thy former, or like intended pranks, shall most terribly and most strangely be plagued,

2 There is a little sparke lies under (that huge heap of ashes) all thine honour, pomp, pride, wealth, and riches, which shall utterly consume all that is uppermost, as it is written.

The Lord, the Lord of Hosts, shall send among his fat ones, leanesse; and under his glory he shall kindle a burning, like the burning of a fire, and the light of *Israel* shall be for a fire, and his holy one for a flame, and it shall burne and devoure his thornes, and his briers in one day.

And shall consume the glory of his Forrest, and of his fruitfull field, both soule and body (*i.e.* this shall be done inwardly and outwardly, and shall be fulfilled both in the history and mystery) and the rest of the trees of his Forrest shall be few, that a childe may write them.

And the Lord, the Lord of Hoasts, shall lop the bough with terror, and the high ones of stature shall be hewen down, and the haughty shall be humbled, And he shall cut down the thickets of the Forrest with iron, and *Lebanon* shall fall by a mighty one, *Isa.* 10.

3 Behold, behold, I have told you.

Take it to heart, else you'l repent every veine of your heart.

For your own sakes take heed.

Its my last warning.

For the cryes of the poore, for the oppression of the needy. For the horrid insolency of proud man, who will dare to sit in my throne, and judge unrighteous judgement.

Who will dare to touch mine Annoynted, and do my Prophets harme.

For these things sake (now) am I arrisen, saith the Lord.
In Auxilium Patris בך

CHAP. V.

1 O *London, London,* my bowels are rolled together (in me) for thee, and my compassions within me, are kindled towards thee.

And now I onely tell thee, that it was not in vaine that this forme hath been brought so farre to thee, to proclaime the day of the Lord throughout thy streets, day and night, for twelve or thirteen dayes together.

And that I have been made such a signe, and a wonder before many of thine Inhabitants faces.

2 Many of them (among other strange exploits) beholding me, fall down flat at the feet of creeples, beggers, lazars, kissing their feet, and resigning up my money to them; being severall times over-emptied of money, that I have not had one penny left, and yet have recruited againe ——

3 And now my hearts! you have been forwardly in all the appearances of God,

There is a strange one (now on foot) judge it not, least you be judged with a vengeance.

4 Turne not away your eyes from it, least you (to your torment) heare this voyce —— *I was a Stranger, and ye tooke me not in.*

Well! bow down before Eternall Majesty, who is universall love, bow down to equality, or free community, that no more of your blood be spilt; that pride, arrogance, covetuousnesse, malice, hypocrisie, self-seeking, &c. may live no longer. Else I tremble at whats comming upon you.

Remember you have been warned with a witnesse.

Deare hearts Farewell.

CHAP. VI.

A terrible word, and fatall blow from the Lord, upon the gathered Churches (so called) especially upon those that are stiled Anabaptists.

1 H E that hath an eare to heare, let him hear what the Spirit saith against the Churches.

Thus saith the Lord: Woe be to thee* *Bethaven,* who callest) thy selfe by the name* *Bethel,* it shall be more tolerable (now in the day of judgement, for *Tyre* and *Sydon,* for those whom thou accountest, and callest Heathens, then for thee.

2 And thou proud *Lucifer,* who exaltest thy self above all

*The house of vanity.
*The house of God.

32

the Stars of God in heaven, shalt be brought down into hell; it shall be more tollerable for *Sodom* and *Gomorrah*, for drunkards and whoremongers, then for thee. Publicans and Harlots shall, Publicans and Harlots do sooner enter into the Kingdome of heaven, then you.

I'le give thee this fatall blow, and leave thee.

3 Thou hast affronted, and defied the Almighty, more then the vilest of men (upon the face of the earth) and that so much the more, by how much the more thou takest upon thee the name of Saint, and assumest it to thy self onely, damning all those that are not of thy Sect.

4 Wherefore be it knowne to all Tongues, Kinreds, Nations, and languages upon earth, That my most Excellent Majesty, the King of glory, the Eternall God, who dwelleth in the forme of the Writer of this Roll (among many other strange and great exploits) hath i'th open streets, with his hand fiercely stretcht out, his hat cockt up, his eyes set as if they would sparkle out; and with a mighty loud voyce charged 100. of Coaches, 100. of men and women of the greater ranke, and many notorious, deboist, swearing, roystering roaring Cavalliers (so called) and other wilde sparks of the Gentry: And have proclaimed the notable day of the Lord to them, and that through the streets of the great Citie, and in Southwark; Many times great multitudes following him up and down, and this for the space of 12. or 13. dayes: And yet (all this while) not one of them lifting up one finger, not touching one haire of his head, or laying one hand on his raiment.

But many, yea many notorious vile ones, in the esteeme of men (yea of great quality among men) trembling and bowing to the God of heaven, &c.

But when I came to proclaim (also) the great day of the Lord (among you) O ye carnall Gospellers.

The Devill (in you) roared out, who was tormented to some purpose, though not before his time.

He there shewed both his phangs and pawes, and would have torn me to pieces, and have eaten me up. Thy pride, envy, malice, arrogance, &c. was powred out like a river of Brimstone, crying out, a Blasphemer, a Blasphemer, away with him: At length threatning me, and being at last raving mad, some tooke hold of my Cloak on one side, some on another, endeavouring to throw me from the place where I stood (to proclaime his Majesties message) making a great uproar in a great congregation of people: Till at length I wrapt up my self in silence (for a season) for the welfavour'd harlots confusion, &c.

And to thine eternall shame and damnation (O mother of

witchcrafts, who dwellest in gathered Churches) let this be told abroad: And let her FLESH be burnt with FIRE.

Amen, Halelujah.

FINIS.

A SECOND

Fiery Flying Roule:

TO

All the Inhabitants of the earth; specially to the rich ones.

OR,

A sharp sickle, thrust in, to gather the clusters of the vines of the earth, because her grapes, are (*now*) fully ripe. And the great, notable, terrible, (yet glorious and joyfull) day of the LORD is come; even the Day of the Lords Recovery and Discovery. Wherein the secrets of all hearts are ripped up; and the secret villanies of the holy Whore, the well-favoured Harlot (who scorns carnall Ordinances, and is mounted up into the notion of Spiritualls) is discovered: And even her flesh burning with unquenchable fire. And the pride of all glory staining.

Together with a narration of various, strange, yet true stories: And severall secret mysteries, and mysterious secrets, which never were afore written or printed.

As also, That most strange Appearance of eternall Wisdome, and unlimited Almightinesse, in choosing base things: And why, and how he chooseth them. And how (most miraculously) they (even base things) have been, are, and shall be made fiery Chariots, to mount up some into divine glory, and unspotted beauty and majesty. And the glory that ariseth up from under them is confounding both Heaven and Earth. With a word (by way of preface) dropping in as an in-let to the new Hierusalem.

These being some things of what are experimented.

Per AUXILIUM PATRIS בך

Howle, rich men, for the miseries that are (just now) coming upon you, the rust of your silver is rising up in judgment against you, burning your flesh like fire, &c.

And now I am come to recover my corn, my wooll, and my flax, which thou hast (theevishly and hoggishly) detained from me, the Lord God Almighty, in the poore and needy.

Also howle thou holy Whore, thou well-favour'd Harlot: for God, and I, have chosen base things to confound thee, and things that are.

And the secrets of all hearts are now revealing by my Gospell, who am a stranger, and besides my selfe, to God, for your sakes. Wherefore receive me, &c. els expect that dismall doom, Depart from me ye cursed, I was a stranger, and ye took me not in.

Printed in the Yeer 1649.

CHAP. I.

The Authors Commission to write, a terrible wo denounced against those that slight the Roule. The Lords claime to all things; together with a hint of a two-fold recovery, wherethrough the most hypocriticall heart shall be ript up.

1. THe Word of the Lord came expressely to me, saying, write, write, write.

2. And ONE stood by me, and pronounced all these words to me with his mouth, and I wrote them with ink in this paper.

3. Wherefore in the Name and Power of the eternall God, I charge thee burn it not, tear it not, for if thou dost, I will tear thee to peices (saith the Lord) and none shall be able to deliver thee; for (as I live) it is the day of my vengeance.

4. Read it through, and laugh not at it; if thou dost I'l destroy thee, and laugh at thy destruction.

5. Thus saith the Lord, though I have been a great while in coming, yet I am now come to recover my corn, and my wool, and my flax, &c. and to discover thy lewdnesse, *Hos.* 2.

Thou art cursed with a curse, for thou hast robbed me (saith the Lord) of my corn, my wool, my flax, &c. Thou hast robbed me of my Tythes, for the Tythes are mine, *Mal.* 3. And the beasts on a thousand hills, yea all thy baggs of money, hayricks, horses, yea all that thou callest thine own are mine.

6. And now I am come to recover them all at thy hands, saith the Lord, for it is the day of my recovery, and the day of my discovery, &c. And there is a two-fold recovery of two

sorts of things, inward, and outward, or civil, and religious, and through both, a grand discovery of the secrets of the most hypocriticall heart, and a ripping up of the bowels of the wel-favoured Harlot, the holy Whore, who scorns that which is called prophanesse, wickednesse, loosenesse, or libertinisme, and yet her self is the mother of witchcrafts, and of all the abominations of the earth.

But more of this hereafter.

7. For the present, I say, Thus saith the Lord, I am come to recover all my outward, or civill rights, or goods, which thou callest thine own.

CHAP. II.

How the Lord will recover his outward things [things of this life] as Money, Corn, &c. and for whom, and how they shall be plagued who detaine them as their owne. Wherein also are some mysticall hints concerning Michaelmasse day, and the Lords day following it this year, as also of the Dominicall letter D. this year.

1. A nd the way that I will walk in (in this great notable and terrible day of the Lord) shall be thus, I will either (strangely, & terribly, to thy torment) inwardly, or els (in a way that I will not acquaint thee with) outwardly, demand all mine, and will say on this wise.

2. Thou hast many baggs of money, and behold now I come as a thief in the night, with my sword drawn in my hand, and like a thief as I am, —— I say deliver your purse, deliver sirrah! deliver or I'l cut thy throat!

3. Deliver MY money to such as* poor despised *Maul* of Dedington in Oxonshire, whom some devills incarnate (insolently and proudly, in way of disdaine) cry up for a fool, some for a knave, and mad-man, some for an idle fellow, and base rogue, and some (truelier then they are aware of) cry up for a Prophet, and some arrant fools (though exceeding wise) cry up for more knave then foole, &c. when as indeed, ther's pure royall blood runs through his veins, and he's no lesse then a Kings son, though not one of you who are devills incarnate; & have your eyes blinded with the God of this world, know it.

For some speciall reason this poor wretch is here instanced.

4. I say (once more) deliver, deliver, my money which thou hast to him, and to poor creeples, lazars, yea to rogues, thieves, whores, and cut-purses, who are flesh of thy flesh, and every whit as good as thy self in mine eye, who are ready to starve in plaguy Goals, and nasty dungeons, or els by my selfe, saith the Lord, I will torment thee day and

night, inwardly, or outwardly, or both waies, my little finger shall shortly be heavier on thee, especially on thee thou holy, righteous, religious *Appropriator*, then my loynes were on *Pharoah* and the Egyptians in time of old; you shall weep and howl for the miseries that are suddenly coming upon you; for your riches are corrupted, &c. and whilst impropriated, appropriated the plague of God is in them.

5. The plague of God is in your purses, barns, houses, horses, murrain will take your hogs, O (ye fat swine of the earth) who shall shortly go to the knife, and be hung up i'th roof, except —— blasting, mill-dew, locusts, caterpillars, yea fire your houses and goods, take your corn and fruit, the moth your garments, and the rot your sheep, did you not see my hand, this last year, stretched out?

You did not see,

My hand is stretched out still.

Your gold and silver, though you can't see it, is cankered, the rust of them is a witnesse against you, and suddainly, suddainly, suddainly, because by the eternall God, my self, its the dreadful day of Judgement, saith the Lord, shall eat your flesh as it were fire, *Jam.* 5.1. to 7.

The rust of your silver, I say, shall eat your flesh as it were fire.

6. As sure as it did mine the very next day after *Michael* the Arch-Angel's, that mighty Angel, who just now fights that terrible battell in heaven with the great Dragon.

And is come upon the earth also, to rip up the hearts of all bag-bearing Judases. On this day purses shall be cut, guts let out, men stabb'd to the heart, womens bellies ript up, specially gammer Demases, who have forsaken us, and imbraced this wicked world, and married *Alexander* the Coppersmith, who hath done me much evill. The Lord reward him, I wish him hugely well, as he did me, on the next day after *Michael* the Arch-Angel.

Which was the Lords day I am sure on't, look in your Almanacks, you shall find it was the Lords day, or els I would you could; when you must, when you see it, you will find the Dominicall letter to be G. and there are many words that begin with G. at this time [GIVE] begins with G. give, give, give, give up, give up your houses, horses, goods, gold, Lands, give up, account nothing your own, have ALL THINGS common, or els the plague of God will rot and consume all that you have.

By God, by my self, saith the Lord, its true.

Come! give all to the poore and follow me, and you shall have treasure in heaven. Follow me, who was numbred among transgressors, and whose visage was more marr'd then any mans, follow me.

CHAP. III

A strange, yet most true story: under which is couched that Lion, whose roaring shall make all the beasts of the field tremble, and all the Kingdoms of the earth quake. Wherein also (in part) the subtilty of the wel-favoured Harlot is discovered, and her flesh burning with that fire, which shall burne down all Churches, except that of the first Born, &c.

1. FOllow me, who, last Lords day Septem. 30. 1649. met him in open field, a most strange deformed man, clad with patcht clouts: who looking wishly on me, mine eye pittied him; and my heart, or the day of the Lord, which burned as an oven in me, set my tongue on flame to speak to him, as followeth.

2. How now friend, art thou poore?

He answered, yea Master very poore.

Whereupon my bowels trembled within me, and quivering fell upon the worm-eaten chest, [my corps I mean] that I could not hold a joynt still.

And my great love within me, (who is the great God within that chest, or corps) was burning hot toward him; and made the lock-hole of the chest, to wit, the mouth of the corps, again to open: Thus.

Art poor?

Yea, very poor, said he.

Whereupon the strange woman who, flattereth with her lips, and is subtill of heart, said within me,

It's a poor wretch, give him two-pence.

But my EXCELLENCY and MAIESTY (in me) scorn'd her words, confounded her language; and kickt her out of his presence.

3. But immediately the WEL-FAVOURED HARLOT [whom I carried not upon my horse behind me] but who rose up in me, said:

"Its a poor wretch give him 6.d. and that's enough for a Squire or Knight, to give to one poor body.

"Besides [saith the holy Scripturian Whore] hee's worse then an Infidell that provides not for his own Family.

"True love begins at home, &c.

"Thou, and thy Family are fed, as the young ravens strangely, though thou hast been a constant Preacher, yet thou hast abhorred both tythes and hire; and thou knowest not aforehand who will give thee the worth of a penny.

"Have a care of the main chance."

4. And thus she flattereth with her lips, and her words being smoother then oile; and her lips dropping as the

honey comb, I was fired to hasten my hand into my pocket; and pulling out a shilling, said to the poor wretch, give me six pence, heer's a shilling for thee.

He answered, I cannot, I have never a penny.

Whereupon I said, I would fain have given thee something if thou couldst have changed my money.

Then saith he, God blesse you.

Whereupon with much reluctancy, with much love, and with amazement [of the right stamp] I turned my horse head from him, riding away. But a while after I was turned back [being advised by my Demilance] to wish him cal for six pence, which I would leave at the next Town at ones house, which I thought he might know [Saphira like] keeping back part.

But [as God judged me] I, as she, was struck down dead.

And behold the plague of God fell into my pocket: and the rust of my silver rose up in judgement against me, and consumed my flesh as with fire: so that I, and my money perisht with me

I being cast into that lake of fire and brimstone.

And all the money I had about me to a penny [though I thought through the instigation of my *quondam Mistris* to have reserved some, having rode about 8. miles, not eating one mouth-full of bread that day, and had drunk but one small draught of drink; and had between 8. or 9. miles more to ride, ere I came to my journeys end: my horse being lame, the waies dirty, it raining all the way, and I not knowing what extraordinary occasion I might have for money.] Yet [I say] the rust of my silver did so rise up in judgement against me, and burnt my flesh like fire: and the 5. of *James* thundered such an alarm in mine ears, that I was fain to cast all I had into the hands of him, whose visage was more marr'd then any mans that ever I saw.

This is a true story, most true in the history.

Its true also in the mystery.

And there are deep ones couch under it, for its a shadow of various, glorious, [though strange] good things to come.

7. Wel! to return —— after I had thrown my rusty canker'd money into the poor wretches hands, I rode away from him, being filled with trembling, joy, and amazement, feeling the sparkles of a great glory arising up from under these ashes.

After this, I was made [by that divine power which dwelleth in this Ark, or chest] to turn my horse head —— whereupon I beheld this poor deformed wretch, looking earnestly after me: and upon that, was made to put off my hat, and bow to him seven times, and was [at that strange posture] filled with trembling and amazement, some sparkles of glory arising up also from under this; as also from under these ashes, yet I rode back once more to the poor wretch, saying, because I am a King, I have done this, but you need not tell any one.

The day's our own.

This was done on the LORDS DAY, Septem. 30. in the year 1649. which is the year of the Lords recompences for Zion, and the day of his vengeance, the dreadfull day of Judgement. But I have done [for the present] with this story, for it is the later end of the year 1649.

CHAP. IV.

How the Author hath been set as a signe and a wonder, as well as most of the Prophets formerly. As also what strange postures the divine Majesty that dwells in his forme, hath set the forme in, with the most strange and various effects thereof upon the Spectators. Also his Communion with the spirits of just men made perfect, and with God the Judge of all, hinted at.

1. IT is written in your Bibles, Behold I and the children whom the Lord hath given me, are for signs and for wonders in Israel, fron the Lord of Hoasts, which dwelleth in Mount Sion, *Isa.* 8.18.

And amongst those who were set thus, *Ezekiel* seems to be higher then the rest by the shoulders upwards, and was more seraphicall then his Predecessors, yet he was the son of *Buzi* (*Ezek.* 1.) which being interpreted is the son of contempt; it pleases me [right well] that I am his brother, a sonne of *Buzi*.

2. He saw [and I in him see] various strange visions; and he was, and I am set in severall strange postures.

Amongst many of his pranks —— this was one, he shaves all the hair off his head: and off his beard, then weighs them in a pair of scales; burns one part of them in the fire, another part hee smites about with a knife, another part thereof he scatters in the wind, and a few he binds up in his skirts, &c. and this not in a corner, or in a chamber, but in the midst of the streets of the great City Hierusalem, and the man all this while neither mad nor drunke, &c. *Ezek.* 5.1.2.3,4. &c. as also in severall other Chapt. amongst the rest, Chap. 12.3. &c. Chap. 4.3. Chap. 24.3. to the end. This *Ezekiel* [to whose spirit I am come, and to an innumerable company of Angels, and to God the Judge of all.]

3. [I say] this great Courtier, in the high Court of the highest heavens, is the son of *Buzi*, a child of contempt on

earth, and set as a sign and wonder (as was *Hosea*, who went in to a whore, &c.) *Hos.* 2. when he (I say) was playing some of his pranks, the people said to him, wilt thou not tell us what these things are to us, that thou dost so, *Ezek.* 24.19. with the 3. verse and so forwards, when he was strangely acted by that omnipotency dwelling in him; and by that eternall, immortall, INVISIBLE (indeed) Majesty, the onely wise God, who dwells in this visible forme, the writer of this Roule, [who to his joy] is numbred amongst transgressors.

4. The same most excellent Majesty (in this forme) hath set the Forme in many strange Postures lately, to the joy and refreshment of some, both acquaintances and strangers, to the wonderment and amazement of others, to the terrour and affrightment of others; and to the great torment of the chiefest of the Sects of Professours; who have gone about to shake off their plagues if they could, some by crying out he's mad, he's drunk, he's faln from grace, and some by scandalising, &c. and onely one, whom I was told of, by threats of caneing or cudgelling, who meeting me full with face, was ashamed and afraid to look on me, &c.

5. But to wave all this.

Because the Sun begins to peep out, and its a good while past day-break, I'l creep forth (a little) into the mystery of the former history, and into the in-side of that strange out-side businesse.

CHAP. V.

The Authors strange and lofty carriage towards great ones, and his most lowly carriage towards Beggars, Rogues, and Gypseys: together with a large declaration what glory shall rise up from under all this ashes. The most strange, secret, terrible, yet most glorious design of God, in choosing base things to confound things that are. And how. A most terrible vial powred out upon the well-favour'd Harlot, and how the Lord is bringing into contempt not only honorable persons, with a vengeance, but all honorable, holy things also. Wholsome advice, with a terrible threat to the Formalists. How base things have confounded base things; and how base things have been a fiery Chariot to mount the Author up into divine glory, &c. And how his wife is, and his life is in, that beauty which makes all visible beauty seem meer deformity.

1. A Nd because I am found of those that sought me not. And because some say, wilt thou not tell us what these things are to us, that thou dost do?

Wherefore waving my charging so many Coaches, so many hundreds of men and women of the greater rank, in the open streets, with my hand stretched out, my hat cock't up, staring on them as if I would look through them, gnashing with my teeth at some of them, and day and night with a huge loud voice proclaiming the day of the Lord throughout London and Southwark, and leaving divers other exploits, &c. It is my good will and pleasure [only] to single out the former story with its Parallels.

2. [*Viz.*] in clipping, hugging, imbracing, kissing a poore deformed wretch in London, who had no more nose on his face, then I have on the back of my hand, [but only two little holes in the place where the nose uses to stand.]

And no more eyes to be seen then on the back of my hand, and afterwards running back to him in a strange manner, with my money giving it to him, to the joy of some, to the afrightment and wonderment of other Spectators.

3. As also in falling down flat upon the ground before rogues, beggars, cripples, halt, maimed; blind, &c. kissing the feet of many, rising up againe, and giving them money, &c. Besides that notorious businesse with the Gypseys and Goal-birds (mine own brethren and sisters, flesh of my flesh, and as good as the greatest Lord in England) at the prison in Southwark neer S. *Georges* Church.

Now that which rises up from under all this heap of ashes, will fire both heaven and earth; the one's ashamed, and blushes already, the other reels to and fro, like a drunken man.

4. Wherefore thus saith the Lord, Hear O heavens, and hearken O earth, Ile overturne, overturne, overturne, I am now astirring the pride of all glory, and bringing into contempt all the honourable of the earth, *Esa.* 23.9. not only honourable persons, (who shall come down with a vengeance, if they bow not to universall love the eternall God, whose service is perfect freedome) but honorable things, as Elderships, Pastorships, Fellowships, Churches, Ordinances, Prayers, &c. Holinesses, Righteousnesses, Religions of all sorts, of the highest strains; yea, Mysterians, and Spirituallists, who scorne carnall Ordinances, &c.

I am about my act, my strange act, my worke, my strange work, that weosoever hears of it, both his ears shall tingle.

5. I am confounding, plaguing, tormenting nice, demure, barren *Mical*, with *Davids* unseemly carriage, by skipping, leaping, dancing, like one of the fools; vile, base fellowes, shamelessely, basely, and uncovered too before handmaids,

---

Which thing was S. *Pauls* Tutor, or else it prompted him to write, God hath chosen BASE things, and things that are despised, to confound —— the things are.——

Well! family duties are no base things, they ar things that ARE: Churches, Ordinances, &c. are no BASE things, though indded Presbyterian Churches begun to live i'th womb, but died there, and rot and stink there to the death of the mother and child. Amen. Not by the Devill, but [by* God] it's true.

Grace before meat and after meat, are no BASE things; these are things that ARE. But how long Lord, holy and true, &c.

Fasting for strife and debate, and to smite with the fist of wickednesse, —— (and not for taking off heavy burthens, breaking every yoke, *Esa.* 58.) and Thanksgiving daies for killing of men for money, are no BASE things, these are things that ARE.

☞ Starting up into the notion of spirituals, scorning History, speaking nothing but Mystery, crying down carnall ordinances, &c. is a fine thing among many, it's no base thing (now adaies) though it be a cloak for covetousnesse, yea, though it be to maintain pride and pomp; these are no base things.

6. These are things that ARE, and must be confounded by BASE things, which *S. Paul* saith, not God hath connived at, winked at, permitted, tolerated, but God hath CHOSEN *&c.* BASE things.

What base things? Why *Mical* took *David* for a base fellow, and thought he had chosen BASE things, in dancing shamelessly uncovered before handmaids.

And barren, demure *Mical* thinks (for I know her heart saith the Lord) that I chose base things when I sate downe, and eat and drank around on the ground with Gypseys, and clip't, hug'd and kiss'd them, putting my hand in their bosomes, loving the she-Gipsies dearly. O base! saith mincing *Mical*, the least spark of modesty would be as red as crimson or scarlet, to hear this.

I warrant me, *Mical* could better have borne this if I had done it to Ladies: so I can for a need, if it be my will, and that in the height of honour and majesty, without sin. But at that time when I was hugging the Gipsies, I abhorred the thoughts of Ladies, their beauty could not bewitch mine eyes, or snare my lips, or intangle my hands in their bosomes; yet I can if it be my will, kisse and hug Ladies, and love my neighbours wife as my selfe, without sin.

7. But thou Precisian, by what name or title soever dignified, or distinguished, do but blow a kisse to thy neighbours wife, or dare to think of darting one glance of one of thine eyes towards her, if thou dar'st.

It's meat and drink to an Angel [who knows none evill, no

44

sin] to sweare a full mouth'd oath, *Rev.* 10.6. It's joy to *Nehemiah* to come in like a mad-man, and pluck folkes hair off their heads, and curse like a devill— and make them swear by God,—— *Nehem.* 13. Do thou O holy man [who knowest evill] lift up thy finger against a Jew, a Church-member, cal thy brother fool, and with a peace-cods on him; or swear I saith, if thou dar'st, if thou dost, thou shalt howl in hell for it, and I will laugh at thy calamity, &c.

8. But once more hear O heavens, hearken O earth, Thus saith the Lord, I have chosen such base things, to confound things that are, that the ears of those [who scorn to be below Independents, yea the ears of many who scorn to be so low as carnall Ordinances, &c.] that hear thereof shall tingle.

9. Hear one word more [whom it hitteth it hitteth] give over thy base nasty stinking, formall grace before meat, and after meat [I call it so, though thou hast rebaptized it—] give over thy stinking family duties, and thy Gospell Ordinances as thou callest them; for under them all there lies snapping, snarling, biting, besides covetousnesse, horrid hypocrisie, envy, malice, evill surmising.

10. Give over, give over, or if nothing els will do it, I'l at a time, when thou least of all thinkest of it, make thine own child the fruit of thy loines, in whom thy soul delighted, lie with a whore— before thine eyes: That that plaguy holinesse and righteousnesse of thine might be confounded by that base thing. And thou be plagued back again into thy mothers womb, the womb of eternity: That thou maist become a little child, and let the mother *Eternity, Almighti-nesse*, who is universall love, and whose service is perfect freedome, dresse thee, and undresse thee, swadle, un-swadle, bind, loose, lay thee down, take thee up, &c.

——And to such a little child, undressing is as good as dressing, foul cloaths, as good as fair cloaths— he knows no evill, &c.— And shall see evill no more,—— but he must first lose all his righteousnesse, every bit of his holinesse, and every crum of his Religion, and be plagued, and confounded [by base things] into nothing.

By base things which God and I have chosen.

11. And yet I shew you a more excellent way, when you have past this. ——In a word, my plaguy, filthy, nasty holinesse hath been confounded by base things. And then [behold I shew you a mystery, and put forth a riddle to you] by base things, base things so called have been confounded also; and thereby have I been confounded into eternall Majesty, unspeakable glory, my life, my self.

12. Ther's my riddle, but because neither all the Lords of the Philistins, no nor my Delilah her self can read it,

I'l read it my self, I'l [only] hint it thus.

Kisses are numbered amongst transgressors —— base things —— well! by base hellish swearing, and cursing, [as I have accounted it in the time of my fleshly holinesse] and by base impudent kisses [as I then accounted them] my plaguy holinesse hath been confounded, and thrown into the lake of fire and brimstone.

And then again, by wanton kisses, kissing hath been confounded; and externall kisses, have been made the fiery chariots, to mount me swiftly into the bosom of him whom my soul loves, [his excellent Majesty, the King of glory.]

Where I have been, where I have been, where I have been, hug'd, imbrac't, and kist with the kisses of his mouth, whose loves are better then wine, and have been utterly overcome therewith, beyond expression, beyond admiration.

13. Again, Lust is numbered amongst transgressors —— a base thing.——

Now faire objects attract Spectators eyes.

And beauty is the father of lust or love.

Well! I have gone along the streets impregnant with that child [lust] which a particular beauty had begot: but coming to the place, where I expected to have been delivered, I have providentially met there a company of devills in appearance, though Angels with golden vialls, in reality, powring out full vialls, of such odious abominable words, that are not lawfull to be uttered.

Words enough to deafen the ears of plaguy holinesse.

And such horrid abominable actions, the sight whereof were enough to put out holy mans eyes, and to strike him stark dead, &c.

These base things (I say) words and actions, have confounded and plagued to death, the child in the womb that I was so big of.

14. And by, and through these BASE things [as upon the wings of the wind] have I been carried into the arms of my love, which is invisible glory, eternall Majesty, purity it self, unspotted beauty, even that beauty which maketh all other beauty but meer uglinesse, when set against it, &c.

Yea, could you imagine that the quintessence of all visible beauty, should be extracted and made up into one huge beauty, it would appear to be meer deformity to that beauty, which through BASE things I have been lifted up into.

Which transcendent, unspeakable, unspotted beauty, is my crown and joy, my life and love: and though I have chosen, and cannot be without BASE things, to confound some in mercy, some in judgement, Though also I have

concubines without number, which I cannot be without, yet
this is my spouse, my love, my dove, my fair one.

Now I proceed to that which followes.

CHAP. VI.

Great ones must bow to the poorest peasants, or els they must rue for it.
No materiall sword, or humane power whatsoever, but the pure spirit of
universall Love, which is the eternall God, can break the neck of
tyranny, oppression, abominable pride, and cruell murder. A
Catalogue of severall judgements recited— as so many warning-
pieces to Appropriators, Impropriators, and anti-free-communic-
ants, &c. The strongest, yea purest propriety that may plead most
priviledge shall suddainly be confounded.

1, $\quad$ A Gain, thus saith the Lord, I in thee, who am eternall
Majesty, bowed down thy form, to deformity.

And I in thee, who am durable riches, command-
ed thy perishable silver to the poore, &c.

Thus saith the Lord,

Kings, Princes, Lords, great ones, must bow to the
poorest Peasants; rich men must stoop to poor rogues, or
else they'l rue for it.

This must be done two waies.

You shall have one short dark hint.

Wil. Sedgewick [in me] bowed to that poor deformed
ragged wretch, that he might inrich him, in impoverishing
himself.

He shall gaine him, and be no great loser himself, &c.

2. Well! we must all bow, and bow, &c. And MEUM must
be converted. —— It is but yet a very little while; and you
shall not say that ought that you possesse is your own, &c.
read *Act.* 2. towards the end, chap. 4.31. to the end, with
chap. 5.1.2. to the 12.

It's but yet a little while, and the strongest, yea, the
seemingly purest propriety, which may mostly plead
priviledge and Prerogative from Scripture, and carnall
reason; shall be confounded and plagued into community
and universality. And ther's a most glorious design in it:
and equality, community, and universall love; shall be in
request to the utter confounding of abominable pride,
murther, hypocrisie, tyranny and oppression, &c. The
necks whereof can never be chopt off, or these villaines ever
hang'd up, or cut off by materiall sword, by humane might,
power, or strength, but by the pure spirit of universall love,

who is the God whom all the world [of Papists, Protestants, Presbyterians, Independents, Spirituall Notionists, &c.) ignorantly worship.

3. The time's coming, yea now is, that you shall not dare to say, your silver or gold is your owne.

It's the Lords.

You shall not say it is your own, least the rust thereof rise up in judgement against you, and burn your flesh as it were fire.

Neither shall you dare to say, your oxe, or your asse is your own.

It's the Lords.

And if the Lord have need of an asse he shall have him.

Or if two of his Disciples should come to unloose him, I wil not [for a 1000. worlds] call them thieves, least the asse should slat my braines out, my bread is not mine own, it's the Lords.

A rogo; to ask. And if a poor Rogue should ask for it—— the Lord hath need of it—— he should have it, least it should stick in my throat and choak me one way or other.

4. Once more, Impropriators! Appropriators! go to, weep and howl, &c. *Jam.* 5.1. to the 7. the rust of your silver shall rise (is rising up) against you, burning your flesh as it were fire, &c.

That is (in a word) a secret, yet sharp, terrible, unexpected, and unsupportable plague, is rising up from under all, that you call your own, when you go to count your money, you shall verily think the Devill stands behind you, to tear you in pieces: You shall not put bread in your mouthes, but the curse shall come along with it, and choke you one way or other. All your former sweets shall be mingled with gall and wormwood: I give you but a hint.

It's the last daies.

5. Well! do what you will or can, know you have been warned. It is not for nothing, that I the Lord with a strong wind cut off (as with a sickle) the fullest, fairest ears of corn this harvest, and drop't them on purpose for the poore, who had as much right to them, as those that (impudently and wickedly, theevishly and hoggishly) stile themselves the owners of the Land.

6. It's not for nothing that such various strange kinds of worms, grubs, and caterpillars (my strong host, saith the Lord of Hosts) have been sent into some graine: Neither is it in vain, that I the Lord sent the rot among so many sheep this last yeer; if they had been resign'd to me, and you had kept a true communion, they had not been given up to that plague.

7. It's not in vain that so many towns and houses have been lately fired over the heads of the Inhabitants: Neither is it in vain, that I the Lord fired the barning and ricks of a Miser in Worcestershire (this yeer) the very same day that he brought in his own, as he accounted it.

On the very same day (I say) his barning and ricks were fired down to the very ground, though multitudes of very expert men in the imployment came to quench it.

Of this the writer of this Scroule was an eye-witnesse.

8. Impropriators! Appropriators! Misers! a fair warning. More of you shall be served with the same sawce.

Others of you I'le deal withall in another way more terrible then this, saith the Lord, till you resign.——

Misers! 'specially you holy Scripturian Misers, when you would say grace before and after meat, read *James* 5.1 to 7. & *Hosea* 2.8,9,10.

CHAP. VII.

A further discovery of the subtilty of the wel-favour'd Harlot, with a Parley between her and the Spirit: As also the horrid villany (that lies hid under her smooth words, in pleading against the Letter and History, and for the Spirit and Mystery, and all for her owne ends) detected. Also upon what account the Spirit is put, and upon what account the Letter. Also what the true Communion, and what the true breaking of bread is.

1. **B**ut now me thinks (by this time) I see a brisk, spruce, neat, self-seeking, fine finiking fellow, (who scornes to be either Papist, Protestant, Presbyterian, Independent, or Anabaptist) I mean the Man of Sin, who worketh with all deceiveablenesse of unrighteovsnesse, 2 *Thes.* 2.

Crying down * carnall ordinances, and crying up† the Spirit: cunningly seeking and setting up himself thereby.

*Downe they must, but no thanks to him. †Up it must, but no thanks to him.

I say, I see him, and have ript up the very secrets of his hearts (saith the Lord) as also of that mother of mischief, that wel-favour'd Harlot, who both agree in one, and say on this wise to me.

2. "Ah! poor deluded man, thou hast spoken of the Wisdome of God in a mystery, and thou hast seen all the history of the Bible mysteriz'd.

"O fool! who hath bewitcht thee, art thou so foolish as to begin in the spirit, and wilt thou now be made perfect in the flesh? keep thee to the spirit, go not back to the letter, keep thee to the mystery, go not back to the history.

A.C.—D

"What? why dost talk so much of *James* 5. and *Hosea* 2. those words are to be taken in the Mystery, not in the History:

"They are to be taken in the Spirit, not as they ile in the Letter."

Thus you have a hint of the neat young mans, and of the well-favour'd Harlots language.

3. But now behold I am filled with the Holy Ghost, and am resolv'd [*Acts* 13.8,9,&c.] to set mine eyes on her and him, (who are no more twaine, but one) and say:

"O full of all subtilty and mischief, thou child of the Devil, thou enemy of all righteousnesse, wilt thou not cease to pervert the right ways of the Lord?

"Be it known to thee, o thou deceitfull tongue, that I have begun in the spirit, and will end in the spirit: I am joyn'd to the Lord, and am one spirit. The spirit's my joy, my life, my strength; I will not let it go, it's my delight.

"The mystery is mine, [mostly] that which I most delight in, that's the Jewel. The historie's mine also, that's the Cabinet. For the Jewels sake I wil not leave the Cabinet, though indeed it's nothing to me, but when thou for thine own ends, stand'st in competition with me for it.

"Strength is mine, so is weaknesse also."

4. I came by water and blood, not by blood only, but by blood and water also.

The inwardnesse is mostly mine, my prime delight is there; the outwardnesse is mine also, when thou for thine own ends, standest in competition with me about it, or when I would confound thee by it.

5. I know there's no Communion to the Communion of Saints, to the inward communion, to communion with the spirits of just men made perfect, and with God the Judge of all.

No other Communion of Saints do I know.

And this is Blood-life-spirit-communion.

6. But another Communion also do I know, which is water, and but water, which I will not be without: My spirit dwells with God, the Judge of all, dwells in him, sups with him, in him, feeds on him, with him, in him. My humanity shall dwell with, sup with, eat with humanity; and why not [for a need] with Publicans and Harlots? Why should I turne away mine eyes from mine own flesh? Why should I not break my bread to the hungry, whoever they be? It is written, the Lord takes care of Oxen.

And when I am at home, I take a great care of my horse, to feed him, dresse him, water him and provide for him.

And is not poor *Maul* of Dedington, and the worst rogue

in Newgate, or the arrantest thief or cut-purse farre better, then a 100. Oxen, or a 1000. such horses as mine?

7. Do I take care of my horse, and doth the Lord take care of oxen?

And shall I hear poor rogues in Newgate, Ludgate, cry *bread, bread, bread, for the Lords sake;* and shall I not pitty them, and relieve them?

Howl, howl, ye nobles, howl honourable, howl ye rich men for the miseries that are coming upon you.

For our parts, we that hear the APOSTLE preach, will also have all things common; neither will we call any thing that we have our own.

Do you [if you please] till the plague of God rot and consume what you have.

We will not, wee'l eat our bread together in singlenesse of heart, wee'l break bread from house to house.

CHAP. VIII.

The wel-favoured Harlots cloaths stript off, her nakednesse uncovered, her nose slit, her hunting after the young man, void of understanding, from corner to corner, fron Religion to Religion, and the Spirit pursuing, overtaking, and destroying her, with a terrible thunder clap ith close, &c.

1. A Nd we wil strip off thy cloaths, who hast bewitch't us, & slit thy nose thou wel-favoured Harlot, who hast (as in many things, so in this) made the Nations of the earth drunk, with the cup of thy fornications: As thus.

Thou hast come to a poor irreligious wretch, and told him he must be of the same Religion as his neighbours, he must go to Church, hear the Minister, &c. and at least once a year put on his best cloaths, and receive the Communion— he must eat a bit of bread, and drink a sip of wine— and then he hath received, &c. he hath been at the Communion.

2. But when he finds this Religion too course for him, and he would faine make after another,

Then immediately thou huntest after him, following him from street to street, from corner to corner, from grosse Protestantisme to Puritanisme, &c. at length from crosse in baptisme, and Common-Prayer-Book to Presbyterianisme, where thou tellest him he may break bread, with all such believers, who believe their horses and their cowes are their own; and with such believers, who have received different light from, or greater light then themselves; branded with the letter B. banished, or imprisoned fourteen weeks together, without bail or main-prise.

3. And here I could tell a large story, that would reach as far as between Oxonshire and Coventrey.

But though it be in the original copy, yet it is my good will and pleasure, out of my great wisdome, to wave the printing of it, and I will send the contents thereof, as a charge and secret plague, secretly into their breasts, who must be plagued with a vengeance, for their villany against the Lord.

Well! to return from this more then needful digression, to the discovery,and uncovering of the wel-favoured Harlot.

Thou hast hunted the young man void of understanding from corner to corner, from religion to religion.

We left him at the Presbyterian —— where such a believer, who believes his horses and his cows are his own, may have his child christned, and may himself be admitted to the Sacrament —— and come to the communion.

And whats that?

Why after a consecration in a new forme, eating a bit of bread, and drinking a sip of wine perhaps once a moneth, why mother of mischief is this Communion?

O thou flattering and deceitfull tongue, God shall root thee out of the Land of the living, is this Communion? no, no, mother of witchcrafts!

5. The true Communion amongst men, is to have all things common, and to call nothing one hath, ones own.

And the true externall breaking of bread, is to eat bread together in singlenesse of heart, and to break thy bread to the hungry, and tell them its their own bread &c. els your Religion is in vain.

6. And by this time indeed thou seest this Religion is in vain.

And wilt therefore hie thee to another, to wit, to Independency, and from thence perhaps to Anabaptisme so called.

And thither the wel-favour'd Harlot will follow thee, and say thou must be very holy, very righteous, very religious.

All other Religions are vain.

And all in the Parish, all in the Countrey, yea all in the Kingdome, and all in the world [who are not of thine opinion] are without, are of the world.

Thou, and thy comrades are Saints.

[O proud devill! O devill of devills! O *Belzebub*!]

Well! [saith she] thou being a Saint must be very holy, and walk in Gospell-Ordinances [saith the wel favour'd Harlot] ay and in envy, malice, pride, covetousnesse, evill surmising, censoriousnesse, &c. also.

And on the first day of the week, when the Saints meet together, to break bread, do not thou omit it upon pain of damnation.

By no means omit it, because thou hast Gospell Ordinances in the purity of them.

—— Papists —— they give wafers. ——

Protestants—— give —— to all ith' Parish tagg ragg, and his fellow if they come.

But we are called out of the world, none shall break bread with us, but our selves, [the Saints together, who are in Gospell Order.]

Besides the Priests of England cut their bread into little square bits, but we break our bread [according to the Apostolicall practise] and this is the right breaking of bread [saith the wel-favour'd Harlot.]

Who hath stept into this holy, righteous Gospell, religious way, [Gospel-Ordinances so called] on purpose to dash to pieces the right breaking of bread: and in the room thereof thrusting in this vain Religion.

7. A Religion wherein *Lucifer* reigns, more then in any.

And next to this in the Independents [so called] both which damn to the pit of hell, those that are a 100. times nearer the Kingdome of heaven then themselves: flattering themselves up in this their vain Religion.

But take this hint before I leave thee.

He that hath this worlds goods, and seeth his brother in want, and shutteth up the bowells of compassion from him, the love of God dwelleth not in him; this mans Religion is in vain.

His Religion is in vain, that seeth his brother in want, &c.

His brother —— a beggar, a lazar, a cripple, yea a cut-purse, a thief ith' goal, &c.

He that seeth such a brother, flesh of his flesh [in want] and shutteth up the bowels of his compassion from him, the love of God dwelleth not in him, his Religion is in vain: and he never yet broke bread —— that hath not forgot his [*meum.*]

9. The true breaking of bread —— is from house to house, &c. Neighbours [in singlenesse of heart] saying if I have any bread, &c. it's thine, I will not call it mine own, it's common.

These are true Communicants, and this is the true breaking of bread among men.

10. And what the Lords Supper is, none know, but those that are continually [not weekly] but daily at it.

And what the true Communion is, those and those only know, who are come to the spirits of just men made perfect, and to God the Judge of all; all other Religion is vain.

Ay, saith the wel-favour'd Harlot [in the young man void of understanding] I see Protestantism, Presbytery, Independency, Anabaptism, are all vain. These coverings are too short, too narrow, too course for me, the finest of these are but harden sheets, and very narrow ones also.

I'l get me some flax, and make me both fine and large sheets, &c. I'l scorn carnall Ordinances, and walk in the Spirit.

Ay, do [saith the wel-favour'd Harlot] speak nothing but mystery, drink nothing but wine, but bloud, thou need'st not eat flesh, &c.

12. And so my young man starts up into the notion of spiritualls, and wraps up a deal of hipocrisie, malice, envy, deceit, dissimulation, covetousnesse, self-seeking in this fine linnen.

Being a hundred fold worse Devills then before.

But now thy villanie, hipocrisie, and self-seeking is discovering, yea discovered to many with a witnesse.

And though the true and pure levelling, is the eternall Gods levelling the Mountains, &c. in man. Which is the
Bloud-Life-Spirit levelling.

Yet the water, or weak levelling, which is base and foolish, shall confound thee.

And hereby, (as also by severall other strange waies, which thou art least of all acquainted withall. I'l discover thy lewdnesse, and shew the rottennesse of thy heart.

I'l call for all to a mite, to be cast into the outward treasury.

And wil bid thee lay down all at my feet, the Apostle, the Lord, And this is a way that I am now again setting up to try, judge, and damne the wel-favour'd Harlot by.

Cast all into the Treasury, &c. account nothing thine owne, have all things in common.

The young man goes away very sorrowfull, —— &c.

The wel-favour'd Harlot shrugs at this. ——

13. When this cometh to passe, a poore wretch whose very bones are gnawn with hunger, shall not go about 13. or 14. miles about thy businesse, and thou for a reward, when thou hast hundreds lying by thee.

I will give thee but one hint more, and so will leave thee.

The dreadful day of Judgement is stealing on thee, within these few hours. Thou hast secretly and cunningly lien in wait, thou hast craftily numbered me amongst transgressors, who to thy exceeding torment, am indeed a friend of Publicans and Harlots.

Thou hast accounted me a devil, saith the Lord.

And I wil rot thy name, and make it stink above ground,

and make thy folly manifest to all men.

And because thou has judged me, I wil judge thee (with a witnesse) expect it suddainly, saith the Lord.

Per AuXILIUM PATRIS כך

A
REMONSTRANCE
OF
The sincere and zealous PROTESTATION
OF
ABIEZER COPPE,
Against the
Blasphemous and Execrable OPINIONS
recited in the ACT of *Aug.* 10, 1650
The breach whereof, the Author hath (through
Mistake) been mis-suspected of, when he hath
not been in the least guilty thereof, &c.

Or, *Innocence* (clouded with the name of
Transgression) wrapt up in silence;
But now (a little) peeping forth from under
the thick and black clouds of Obloquie,

Arising out of the sea of Malice in some, and out
of Weakness, Ignorance, and Mistake in others; who
are by the Author much pitied, and dearly beloved. And for
their sakes primely, as also for the satisfaction of
many, and information of all.

This ensuing
Remonstrance, Vindication, and *Attestation*
is published,

Per me,   Abiezer Coppe,   *— de Newgate.*

Which is as a Preamble to a farther future Declaration
of what he hath been, and now is; who hath
been so cloathed with a cloud, that few have known him.

London, Printed by JAMES COTTREL. 1651.

*Some said He is a good man; others said, Nay but he is mad, and
hath a devil.*
*He is a wine-bibber, a glutton and a drunkard; a friend of publicans
and harlots.*
But wisdom is justified of her children.

*All fleshly
interests, carnal
Gospellers, and
pretenders to
Religion, with
some secret
enemies (through
seeming friends)
to the State,
combining
together to incense
them against me,
because I have
faithfully and
boldly declaimed
against their
hypocrisie, pride,
covetousness, self-
seeking, and
villany, covered
under the cloak of
fleshly holiness
and Religion, &c.
†Which were
put out half a
year after mine
imprisonment.

I Having patiently, cheerfully, and silently sustained (*through the malice, ignorance, mistake, and blinde zeal of Informers) a tedious twelve-months imprisonment in the common Goals of *Warwick*, *Coventry*, and that most infamous Goal of *Newgate*, Have been within these few days informed by my dearest friend, That

The two†Acts of *May* 10. and *Aug.* 9. 1650 were put out because of me; thereby secretly intimating that I was guilty of the breach of them. Whereupon, (after my long, and by many admired patience and silence) I thought good not so much for mine own sake, (for my pure innocence supports me, and lifts up my head above all these things) but for the sake of others,

To present

This ensuing Remonstrance, Vindication and Attestation; Resolving, by the help of the Omnipotent, Omnipresent JEHOVAH (whom I purely *worship in the spirit* having *no confidence in the flesh*) to enlarge my self (when I enjoy my liberty) upon these things; and to all unprejudiced spirits (and perhaps to the silencing of them also) to give an account of my self, in reference to those Various Dispensations past and present, that I have been and am led into and thorow: as also, the removing of all stumbling-blocks, the clearing up of those mistakes, and the wiping away those aspersions, which (through malice, weakness, ignorance, and mistake) have been cast upon me; who have been so covered with a cloud, that not one amongst a thousand know me.

But for the present, I shall adress myself to the Acts; and begin with that of *Aug.* 9.

In the Preamble of this Act the Parliament express their desires (**by all GOOD MEANS) to propogate the Gospel** *&c*. Which is the desire of my soul. And it is always my fervent prayer to Him whose it is, That He *the Prince of peace*, (whose *burden is easie*, and whose *yoke is light*; who *ruleth in righteousness*; who *judgeth not according to outward appearance, but judgeth righteous judgement*) that he would, by his own out-stretched Arm, set it up. And I resolve never to give mine eyes any rest, till I see it flourish: for it is my Life.

They farther express

Their desire to suppress (**Prophaneness and Wickedness, Superstition and Formality,** *&c*.)

The two former, my soul abhors, and I hate them with a perfect hatred; and have, by Life and Conversation, by Doctrine and Example (for many yeers) decried them; yea, even since I have been by all men (except those that knew me) cried up (as my *fore-runner* before me was by all sorts even of the most religious and righteous men, except a handful that knew him) for the worst of sinners, the vilest of persons; for a *Blasphemer, a Devil* &c.

And as for *Idolatory, Superstition, and Idolatrous Formality*; Have any been a *Boanerges* upon this account? (I speak as a fool.) I have thundered more against them then they all. And for my zeal herein, and against finer and subtiller pieces of Formality, the coals were first kindled against me. And now the fire is at the highest: whereat I laugh; having sweet union and communion with the Father and the Son; living in that Kingdom wherein dwelleth righteousness and peace; triumphing in *joy unspeakable, and full of glory*: sweet Peace and pure Content being my continual repast.

Neither do I repent,

That the Almighty (whose I am, and who will do with his own what he pleaseth) Hath set me (as formerly he hath most of his Holy Prophets and Servants) as *A SIGNE and a WONDER. — And —— as a stumbling stone, and ROCK of OFFENCE to both the Houses of Israel*, &c,

But to proceed.

The Act is bent against these ensuing Execrable Opinions &c. As (first) [**The denial of the necessity of Civil and Moral righteousness amongst men.**]

If there are such a generation of men, they stand or fall to their own master. As for me, I say concerning them, *O my soul! come not thou into their secrets: unto their assemblies, mine honour, be not thou united*, Gen. 49.6.

This Opinion (in the presence of the All-seeing God, in whose presence I am, and whom I serve) I utterly protest against. And in the same presence, I most joyfully (to his praise) affirm, That that Golden Law, which is the Basis of all Civil and Moral righteousness among men; (Viz. *Whatsoever ye would that men should do unto you, even so do you to them*, &c.) is by the finger of God (in indelible letters) written as a Law of Life in my heart.

And here I can boldly (as in reference to the grace of God) though in all humility (as in reference to my self) challenge the whole world, and say, *Whose ox have I taken? or whose ass have I taken? or to whom have I done any wrong?* Whom have I dealt unjustly with? where is ever a drop of blood that I have shed? whom have I defrauded of a shoo-latchet or a thred? *&c.*

Herein do I make my boast of God all the day long, and in him do I triumph and rejoyce, though I am (to my joy also) numbered amongst Transgressors, and the chiefest of them preferred before me; many of them being released, and *set at liberty; and I (patiently and silently) lie by the

*Isa. 8.18, 14, 15. Zech. 8.3, 8.
☞ [Men wondered at.] *Their words wondered at, their carriage wondered at, their actions wondered at*, &c.
*As was Hosea, Hos. 1.2.

*At which I envie not, &c. but take notice of, as do some hundreds also besides me.

walls, as having a visage more marred then any man's, &c.
But I proceed,
And avowedly protest, that I hate and detest, yea (in the presence of God) protest against all those blasphemous Opinions or Tenents recited in page 980, from the thirteenth line thereof to the seven and twentieth line of pag.981. And many, or most of them, I will particularly hint at;
As primely this.

I do not **vainly, ignorantly, and blasphemously affirm** my **self, or any other meer creature, to be very God**: neither was this Tenent (or any of the rest that follow) ever mine.

But this I have and do affirm, and shall still upon the house tops affirm, and shall expire with the wholesom sound, and orthodoxal opinion That God Christ is in the creature.

[——— CHRIST IN YOU except you are reprobates, 1 Cor.]
The contrary assertion is the Blasphemie of Blasphemies, &c.

Again, I disavow, disown, detest, and protest against that Opinion which holdeth, That [**God dwelleth in the creature, and nowhere else,** &c.] I live in that sound and orthodox opinion of Omnipresencie; of which I can speak feelingly knowingly powerfully: whereof I formerly (in the time of mine own righteousness, which was *as menstrous rags*; and in time of my fleshly wisdom, which was *enmity to God*) spake of formally, ignorantly, notionally (onely) like a Parot in a Cage.

*Isai
*I Cor

And as for **the Righteousness, Holiness of God,** &c.. I had rather be cut to pieces then speak against it: for it is my Life. And whatever I have spoken against Righteousness and Holiness, it hath been against that Righteousness of Man, which is *as menstruous rags* &c. and against that carnal mock-holiness, *pseud*-holiness of man which is a cloak for all manner of Villany; upon which the vengeance of God is and hath been poured forth &c.

*Isai

And as for **Uncleanness, prophane Swearing, Drunkenness, Filthiness, Brutishness, &c**. I declaim against them, as unholy &c.

As also, for **Lying, Stealing, Cozening, and defrauding others,** my soul abhors.

Further, I hold, declare and maintain, that **Murther, Adultery, Incest, Fornication, Uncleanness, Sodomie, &c**. are things sinful, shameful, wicked, impious, and abominable, in any person, &c.

Or that **Heaven and Happiness consisteth in the acting of these or such things;** and the rest, as they follow in pag.981, are things that I disown, disavow, and protest against.

I shall conclude with this Affirmation and Asseveration:

That there is Heaven, and Hell; Salvation, and Damnation. Heaven for all those that repent of their sins, that *cease to do evil, and learn to do well.* Heaven, for all them that are washt, purged, and cleansed, by the Spirit of our God. Heaven, for all them that have Christ, the King of Glory, Eternal Majestie, in them. And Hell, and Damnation, to all that *touch the apple of his eye,* that oppose *the Lords Anointed,* and that *do his Prophets any harm.*

It was in my thoughts to have said something concerning the Act of *May* 10; but, upon reading thereof, I see nothing in it but what is contained in that of *August*; and therefore my labour is saved.

And I shall onely adde a word or two concerning Liberty and Community.

As for Liberty, I own none but *the glorious liberty of the sons of God* which I and *the whole creation groans* after. And I do from my heart detest and protest against all Sinful liberty, or that is destructive to soul or body.

And as for Community, I own none but that Apostolical, Saint-like Community spoken of in the Scriptures. So far I either do or should own Community, that if flesh of my flesh be ready to perish, I either will or should call nothing that I have mine own: if I have bread, it shall or should be his; else all my Religion is vain. I am for dealing bread to the hungry, for cloathing the naked, for the *breaking of every yoke,* for the *letting of the oppressed go free.* I am or should be as my heavenly Father, who is kinde to all, loving to all, even to the ungodly, &c. *Mat. 6.* I can (through grace) pity those that are objects of compassion, and out of my poverty and penury relieve those that are in want. *And if this be to be vile,* —— &c.

Yet,

Know all men by these Presents, That I am utterly against that Community which is sinful, or destructive to soul or body.

Ita testor, ABIEZER COPPE.

POSTSCRIPT

I Have onely one word more, and for the present I have done. There are several Pamphlets extant against a People called RANTERS; two whereof bear this Inscription in their brazen foreheads, [Published by Authority] *else the malice and simplicity of the Pamphleter should have been still laugh'd at onely, and yet (upon another account) pitied by me.*

For the present, I will onely give —— to understand, That the Pamphlets are scandalous, and bespattered with Lyes and Forgeries, in setting me in the front of such actions which I never did, which my soul abhors; such things which mine eyes never beheld, such words which my tongue never spake, and mine ears never heard.

All like that false aspersion, —— Viz. that I was accompanied to Coventry with two she-disciples, and that I lay with two women there at once. Which two she-disciples were Captain Beak, and other Souldiers, who have hurried me from Goal to Goal; where I sing Hallelujahs to the righteous Judge, and lie in his bosome, who is everlasting loving kindness. Amen.

HALLELUJAH.

FINIS.

Copp's Return

to the wayes of TRUTH:
IN A
Zealous and Sincere PROTESTATION
Against Severall Errors;
And in a
Sincere and zealous TESTIMONY
to severall Truths:
OR,
Truth asserted against, and triumphing over *Error*,
And the Wings of the

Fiery flying Roll clipt, &c.

BY

ABIEZER COPPE,

---

the [supposed] Author of the Fiery flying Roll.

Herein is also something hinted concerning the *Author*, in
reference to the sinfulness and strictness of his Life.

With a little t'uch of what he hath been, and now is;
Sparkling here and there throughout these Lines,
And in the Preface.

Also a Letter of Mr *Durie's*, with several Proposals
of great concernment, hereunto since annexed:
And by the aforesaid Author (*A.C.*) faithfully, & fully answered, &c.

---

*I have seen the wickedness of folly, and the foolishness
of madness. And now I apply my heart to
wisdome. Ecclei.*
JOSUAH *the High Priest [was] cloathed with filthy
garments. And the Angel saith, take away the
filthy garments from him, and set a mitre on his
head —— Zech.3.*

London, Printed by *Tho. Newcomb.* 1651.

THE CONTENTS.

IV. The Conclusion.

Some principal things in the second part (or Answer to M. Durie's Proposals, contained.

THE prime and principal motives inducing me to desire my enlargement:
    1. What Sin is.
    2. That sin is sin; whether men imagin it to be so, or no.
    3, & 4. That men do not please God as well when they sin, as when they sin not.
    5. Some things concerning the Law of God.
    6. Concerning God, and the souls of men, &c.
    How we are partakers of the Divine Nature: wherein is something hinted concerning our spiritual filiation. And concerning our spiritual and mystical fraternity and union with Christ.
    7. Something concerning the Resurrection of the body, and the last Judgement.

TO THE

Supream Power,
THE

PARLIAMENT

of the Common-wealth of
ENGLAND;
And to the Right Honourable the
COUNCEL of STATE,

appointed by their Authority.

Right Honourable,

I *Am exceedingly sorry, that I am fallen under your honours displeasure.*

And the rather because I am perswaded that you take no delight to lay heavy burthens upon any, nor to afflict any above measure.

And although I have FORMERLY wondered at my sore, tedious, and long continued imprisonment, under which unsupportable burthen I extreamly groan.

And the rather in respect of my poor weak disconsolate wife: (whom, I left in perfect health and strength) and my small innocent children.

She being brought (almost) to deaths dore, with continual and sore anguishing for my tedious imprisonment.

And for the space of above half a year, and to this day is under the Physitians hand, to our great Grief and charge:

Besides that unspeakable and continual charge (which in several respects) I lie at, and for the space of a year and half have lien at in prison.

Which hath wasted and almost utterly undone mine and me, that I have scarce clothes to hang on my back.

And all that little that I have at home, ruined and spoiled, &c.

And my poor innocent children scattered here and there in several places, to our great care, Grief, and charge.

Although I say I have formerly wondered at the tediousnesse, and long continuation of my imprisonment, yet in all humility, I stoop to, and humbly acknowledg your Justice. And do not (now) much admire at my imprisonment.

First, in that, I have been so slow, slack, and negligent in making any addresses to you.

Which indeed I resolved not to do: neither could I at all do it, til whatsoever came from me, came [Ex intimis medullis] *from my very soul and heart: as these —— that I now humbly present you withall do.*

And secondly, because I am given to understand, that your Honours have been extreamly laden, and your ears filled brim full of complaints against me* which have arose from a kinde of zeal in some, from inveterate malice in others.

From ignorance, weakness, mistake, misapprehensions, and misunderstandings in others.

Which hath been occasioned by some bypast, and indeed, strange actions and carriages. And by som difficult, dark, hard, strange, harsh, and almost unheard of words, and expressions of mine.

Of which I shall make bold to give, first your honours, and then the *world a brief account.

And if you please,

[Thus]

With this introduction,

And a touch of what, and where I have been afore this strange appearance.

[Thus]

As the Lord of old took fleshly Israel by the hand, and led them from place to place: pitching and removing their Tents (from place to place) hundreds of times (for the space of 40. years together) in the wilderness &c.

So hath he took me by the hand, &c.

And hath transacted and done over the same things (in a spiritual sence) pitching and removing my tents from place to place.

Setting, and seating me in various forms.

In all which I have lived and acted zealously and conscientiously. Never stirring a foot, till I clearly apprehended this voice (All along.)

*Arise, get thee hence, remove thy Tent, &c. to such a place, &c.

And so removing me from grosser, and impurer, to finer and purer forms, &c.

And at length he set me, and seated me in that——

Which is (now) most in request; though it hath formerly been muchly opposed: and they of that way persecuted.

And for which I my self have (some years since, to my joy and comfort) sustained a 14 weeks close imprisonment, even for that way, which did, and now doth, fling dirt in the face of all other waies —— affirming all other —— to be false waies, and worships. And that onely to be the Gospel way, back'd on with many presidents and precepts, and plain texts of Scripture.

When I dwelt there —— I walked most zealously, and most

conscientiously: and I then shined gloriously in the eyes of many hundreds, who lived with me in that Region.

But at length, I did for a season leave that way: and thought tha. I was shewn a more excellent way, living and triumphing in joy unspeakable, and full of glory, in the power, spirit, and life of tha which I was groaping after in the figure, flesh, form, and outside &c. I was fed* with such dainties, that the tongue of men & angels cannot express.

*Viz, I was abundantly satisfied with the loving kindness of the Lord, &c. (which was clearly, purely, and freely manifested to me) and with the light of his countenance, &c. living in peace, joy, and glorious consolation. And the Lord by his spirit (in his word) revealing and opening to me many glorious things which I neither saw nor understood afore, &c.

Unfathomable, unspeakable mysteries and glories, being clearly revealed to me.

Past finding out by any human search, or its sharpest discernings, &c.

But at length the terrible, notable day of the Lord, stole upon me unawares, like a thiefe in the night.

Even that DAY burst in upon me, which burneth like an oven, and NO FLESH, (no not the FLESH of FOWLES which sore aloft, can stand before it, Malach. chap.3. and chap.4.

So that I can very well take up Habbacuks *expresse,*

Hab.3. when I saw him.——

My bowles trembled, my lipps quivered, rottenness entered into my bones, &c.

Why?

Before him came the Pestilence, and burning coales at his feet &c.

**And the cup of the Lords right hand, was put into mine hand* &c.

*Hab.2.

**And it was filled brim full of intoxicating wine, and I drank i. off, even the dreggs thereof.*

*which was the righteous judgement of the Lord, &c. upon me.
    O the height! and depth! and length! and breadth!— how unsearchable are his ways! and his judgements past finding out, *Rom*

Whereupon being mad drunk, I so strangely spake, and acted . knew not what.

To the amazement of some.

To the sore perplexity of others.

And to the great grief of others.

For I was (really, in very deed) besides my self.

And till that cup passed from me, I knew not what I spake or did.

And because I was as rich, and as great as Nebuchadnezza *was; I was therefore to be served, as he was.*

Sure I am, (in a sense) I was.

In a spiritual sense: I was as rich, (I say) and as great as Nebuchadnezzar, *and as full as proud as he.*

Wherefore I'le (a little) dive into the mystery of that History Dan.4.

For me thinks it is showen to me that, that hits me——

In a mystical sense, I built a great Babel.

And (in the pride of my heart) I walking in the Palace of the Kingdome of Babylon, *i.e. recreating, and priding my self, in the pleasures of (that which I now see to be* בבל*) Babel, i.e. confusion.*

68

I said, is not this great Babel, which I have built, &c. whereupon my KINGDOME was taken from me.

And I was driven from MEN, Dan. 4.32.

———From MEN,

i.e. That pure spark of Reason, (was for a season) taken from me. And I driven from it; from men, from RATIONALITY; from PURE humanity, &c.

And thus was I driven from MEN.

And have been with the beasts of the field, Dan. 4.32,33.

I have been with BEASTS.

I have fed with BEASTS, &c.

I have eaten GRASSE with OXEN.

Have been conversant with BEASTS.

And have been company for BEASTS, &c.

And sure I am, (a) my hairs were grown like EAGLES feathers; and my nails like Birds CLAWES. (a) Dan. 4.33.

And (now I am come to my self) I know it, and divers will know, (as many have felt) what I mean. ———

But these daies are ended, Dan. 4.34.

And I have lifted up mine eyes to Heaven.

And mine UNDERSTANDING is returned unto me. And I blesse the most high, and praise, and honour him that liveth for ever; whose dominion, is an everlasting dominion. And his kingdome is from generation, to generation.

(b) And all the inhabitants of the EARTH, are reputed as nothing. And he doth according to his will in the Army of Heaven, and among the inhabitants of earth. (b) Dan 4.35.

And none can stay his hand, or say to him, what dost thou?

(c) And now I praise, and extoll, and honour the King of Heaven, ALL whose works are truth, and his waies judgement: and those that walk in pride, he is able to abase, &c. (c) Dan. 4.37

And now since, mine UNDERSTANDING is returned to mee.

I will dwell with my WIFE, as a man of knowledge:

I will love my little CHILDREN.

I will love all my BRETHREN, though of different statures, ages, and complexions, &c.

My strong Brethren, and my weak also, I will not offend.

My sickly ones I will pity, and visit, and be serviceable to them.

And my babe brethren, I will dandle on my knee; and do the best I can to quiet them, when they cry, and are crabbed, &c.

And with my brethren that are at age, I will dine and sup; with them I will talk and conferre.

With them I will eat, drink, and be merry in the Lord.

But I will hasten to a Conclusion,

Knowing that prolixity is not sutable to such personages, as your Honours are.

I will give but one hint: and I have done ———

I have been (a long while) cloathed with filthy garments, and have lien in the channel.

Every one that hath past by me, have cast dirt upon me.

And I have lien still.

But now (in THESE ——) I shake off the dirt, rags and all.

And I appear to your Honours, and to the world, in such an habit, as my penury will afford me.

I have patiently, and silently heard my self accounted, the father of mischief: and the grand authour of errors.

In many things I have been injuriously dealt withal: and several reports have gone of me, which have not been (in the least degree) true.

However, I have given offence to many, and grieved others:

For which, my heart akes, my soul is grieved, and my bowels are kindled with compassionate tendernesse, and tender compassion towards them.

There are many* spurious brats, lately born: and because their parents have looked upon me as a rich Merchant, they have took on them the boldnesse to lay them at my door, &c.

Some of them (indeed) look somewhat like my children.

But however, to put all out of doubt,

Whether they are mine, or no: I will not be so full of foolish pity, as to spare them.

I will turn them out of doors, and starve them to death.

And as for those which I know are not mine own: I will be so holily cruel, as to dispatch them.

*I'll take those children young,

And dash their bones, against hard stones,

That lie the streets among.

And as for my self,

Although I have been strangely acted,

☞ *And by the Devil deluded,*

Yet if I might gain a Kingdom, I could neither act, nor speak as I have done.

But I am resolved (by the grace of God) to give no offence (either in life, or doctrine) to any.

But both by life and doctrine, will decrie, whatsoever hath occasioned out-cries against me. And hath offended God, your Honours, and grieved others. And I pray, hope, and believe, (that through the grace of God) my future deportment, to all sorts, shall make amends for what is by past.

These, with my self, I lay prostrate at your Honours feet:
  For I am,

Right Honourable,

From the House of Bondage, where I live in favour of the Prince of Peace.
————NEWGATE

Your humble, and faithful servant, and very, very poor prisoner

May 30
The day of my Nativity, 1619
And the day of my new birth. 1651

And,
Loving and peaceful to all men.

ABIEZER COPPE.

Truth asserted against,
AND
TRIUMPHING
OVER
ERROR.

Now I will lay the Axe to the root of the Tree, even to this grand Error, (viz.) This

I. ERROR.
That there is no sinne.

Concerning this Error,
1. I disown, detest, and protest against it.
2. I assert and prove the contrary (*viz*)

I. ASSERTION.

I Assert, and prove,
That there is sinne:
For, there is not a just man upon Earth, that doth good, and sinneth not, as it is written, *Ecclesiast. 7.20.*

Every man on earth, living here below, sinneth: is [ἀμαρπλθ , i.e.] a sinner, a sinner all over: full, brim-full of sin.

And of sinners, I am the chief.

And this (with unspeakable grief, sorrow of soul, and anguish of Spirit) I began to see in my tender years, when my heart melted like wax before the Lord.

And because I have been set as a Beacon on a hill, it will not be amiss to speak something concerning myself, in reference to sin. [And the rather because by wofull experience, I know as much as any man in the world, that there is sin, and what is sin.

And how, and wherein I have sinned; and what it hath cost me.

All which will illustrate this assertion —— which I will mostly dwell upon The contrary *Error* being the ground and Foundation of all the *Errors* which many suppose I am (or rather have been)* poysoned withall.]

But to leave this *Parenthesis,* and to return to what I was saying.

When I was about 13 years old, sin began to lie at the dore.

*If I have drunk any deadly poyson it can do me no harm. *Mar.* 16.18. THE Physition hath given me a pure purge, and a powerful antitidote, &c.

72

The sight whereof was the Resurrection of several passions in me: as hatred, fear, grief, &c. And I began to flie from it, as from the face of a Serpent: arming my self against it, as against the deadliest enemy: setting a strict guard: making the watch as sure as I could.

Watching my thoughts, my actions; and watching my words, that I might not* *offend with my tongue.*

*Psal.39.

Whereupon I writ upon Scrouls of Parchment, this inscription, [*Yea yea, nay, nay.*]

And sewed them about my rists.

So far was I, even from [*Faith, and Troth Oaths:*] From petty Oaths, or the least appearance of evill and sinfull speaking that if I heard any one say, [*O Lord, O Christ, O God,* &c.] upon any triviall occasion, my flesh trembled thereat, it was even as a dagger to my heart.

And God is my Record, that in 27 years space, no such word proceeded out of my mouth.

I looking upon [*O Christ, O God,* &c.] as a great breach of that pure Commandment, which saith, *Thou shalt not take the name of the Lord thy God in vain,* &c.

*Exod.20.

And from the age of 13. and so forward, I began to take and keep a dayly Register of my sins, and set them down in a Book.

And in my evening and midnight prayer, (prayer by heart so called) I did constantly in that part of prayer called *Confession,* (with grief of soul, sighs and groans, and frequently with tears) confess over my sins.

When none eye saw me, but his that searcheth the heart, and tryeth the reins: and when no ear heard me but his that made the ear.

I also tryed my self for several years together, to read 9.6. and at least 3 chapters in the Bible every day: and much of the Scripture did I learn by heart.

I was in private, and most secret Fasting often.

Tears were my drink: dust and ashes my meat.

And sack-cloth my clothing.

Zeal, Devotion, and exceeding strictness of life and conversation, my life.

Neither is there, or was there any (even the highest and strictest) way of Religion, but I have zealously walked in it, as many hundreds can bear me witness.

But all this while I could not, neither to this day, can I see any thing in my self but sin.

And all my prayers tears, sighs, groans, watchings, fastings, humilliations, &c. besmeared over with filth and uncleanness.

And in the presence of the heart-searcher, and

rein-tryer, I speak it: I have wept over my tears, because I could weep not more: not better, &c.

And have been greatly humbled for my humiliation, because it was not greater, not better.

And asham'd of all, because sin hath clinged so close to them all.

Besides those innumerable sinfull thoughts, words and deeds, which have invironed me about on every side.

This that I have now hinted in reference to the strictness of my life, is not blowing a Trumpet in mine own praise——

I have felt it like pangs of death: I speak it with sorrow and shame: and all to this purpose,

That I might proclaim, *There is sin, sin with a witness.*

And now do *I* lift up* my voice like a Trumpet, herein do I cry aloud, and spare not my self.

*Isa. 58.1. to the 8 verse.

Nor - to shew the house of *Jacob* their sins, &c.

And if the righteous scarcely be saved; where shall the sinner and ungodly appear?

If our prayers, tears, sighs, groans, huniliations, [take all i'th'lump -] righteousness can scarcely be saved,- *justified* in themselves, &c. where shall our stark staring wickednesses, &c. appear?

　　　O Sin! Sin! Sin!

　　　There is Sin.

Murther, Theft, Adultery, Drunkenness, Swearing, Cursing, Uncleanness, Uncleanness, Covetousness, Pride, Cruelty, Oppression, Hypocrisie, Hatred, Envy, Malice, Evil surmising, is sin.

Nothing but villany, sin, and transgression in me, the chief of sinners.

In man ——

In every man.

There is none righteous; no, not one.

None that do good; no, not one.

All are Sinners.

Thieves, little thieves, and great thieves, drunkards, adulterers, and adulteresses. Murtherers, little murtherers, and great murtherers. All are Sinners. Sinners All.

[*Rom.* 3. from the 9. to the 21. *verse.*]

What then. Are we better then they?

No, in no wise.

—— *All are under sin.*

As is written, there is none righteous; no, not one; - there is none that doth good; no, not one.

Their throat is an open sepulchre, with their tongues, they have used deceit. The poyson of asps is under their lips.

Their mouth is full of cursing, and bitterness.

Their feet are swift to shed bloud.

Destruction, and misery, are in their ways.

THE WAY of PEACE, have they not known.

Now we know, that what things soever the Law saith, it saith to them that are under the Law; that every mouth may be stopped; and all the world may become guilty before God.

Therefore by the DEEDS of the Law, shall no flesh be justified in his fight, &c.

But NOW the righteousness of God WITHOUT the LAW is manifest ——But

[Verse, 23.] —— *ALL* have sinned, *&c.*

Verse 21. *All* the world [*is*] become guilty before God.

Guilty, guilty, my Lord!

All are full of sin.

I, —— and the Nation.——

Ah! sinfull I.

*Ah! sinful nation. A people laden with iniquity from the sole of the foot even to the HEAD: there is no soundness in it: but wounds, and bruises, and putrifiing sores.

     To what purpose is the multitude of your sacrifices to me saith the Lord? &c.

When you come to appear before me, who hath required these things at your hands, &c?

The new Moons and Sabbaths, the calling of ASSEMBLIES, I cannot away with: it is INIQUITY, even the solemn meeting: And when you spread forth your hands, I will hide mine eyes from you: yea, when you make many prayers, I will not hear.

Your hands are full of bloud.

How is the faithfull City become an harlot? It was full of judgement, righteousness lodged in it, but now murtherers.

The Princes are rebellious, and companions of Thieves:

EVERY ONE loveth gifts, and followeth after rewards -

[But] I will restore thy Judges as at the first, &c.

[And] Zion shall be redeemed with JUDGEMENT, &c.

And, now[†]O my God, I am ashamed, and blush to lift up my face, to thee my God. For we have sinned.

We, our Kings, our Rulers. Our Priests, our Judges.

All have sinned, and gone astray.

Do sin, are sinners.

Wo be to us, we are sinners.

Wo be to the inhabitants of the Earth——

The EARTH is full of sin.

There is sin, sin with a witness.　　　　*Ita testor*

ABIEZER COPPE.

*Isa. 1.4.5.6.7. 10.11.12. 13.14.15. 21.23.24. 26.27.

†*Ezra9. Dan:9:*

Let this suffice for the first assertion,
That there is sin.

And let this, as also divers other things in the following *Assertions*, serve as sharp shears to clip the wings of the *Fiery flying Role*: which insinuats several blasphemous opinions, and which insinuats that nothing is otherwise a sin, then as men imagine it to themselves to be so: Which – I utterly disown, and protest against, (as may be more fully seen in my answer to Mr. *Duries* Proposal to me concerning sin, *&c.*)

Wherefore I say, let the wings of the *Fiery flying Role*, be clipt (by this large Tract concerning sin, and by that which follows; with my answer to Mr. *Dury*) and let it be thrown headlong into its own place, the Lake of fire and brimston, and the great Abyss from whence it came.

And let me mourn that I and the whole world lie in darkness, and are involved in   *Sin and wickedness.*

II. ERROR.
That there is no God.

C Oncerning this *Error*,
First, I utterly disown, detest, and protest against it, as a horrid blasphemous opinion.

And although I have been slanderously reported of in this particular (as in divers others) yet I challenge the whole world to prove or affirm to my face, that ever I affirmed any such thing.

Yea, I can with joy, and boldness (in the presence of the *All-seeing God*) affirm, that I never said it in my heart, much less with my mouth,
That there is no God.

II. ASSERTION.
[But on the contrary I affirm and know]
That there is a God.

*Jo.4.

*Concerning this, see more at large in that piece of *Hierogliphical* Divinity, in the preface to *Rich. Coppins* book.

A Nd* God is a *Spirit*, having his being in himself; yea, he is that [*Ens entium*] that *being of beings*, as that Sacred and unfathomable word [יהוה] *Jehovah*, [from הוה] imports.

He is the [*Summum bonum,*] *the chiefest good.*

The fountain of life and light.

He is the *Alpha*, and *Omega*, the first and the last, the begining and the ending, *&c.*

He is said to be the God of Love & peace,
[*Phil.*4. *Rom.*15.]
And a man of War.   [*Exod.*15.]
The Lyon, and Lamb. [*Revel.*5.]
The Branch, and Root. [*Isa.*11. with *Rev.*22.]
A jealous God.   [*Exod.*20.]
And the God of mercies.   [1 *Cor.*]
    And all these (seemingly) cross denominations, do
finely, and secretly declare him to be ALL, in ALL, according
to the Scriptures, 1 *Cor.*15.28. Colos.3.11.
    The heavens and firmament; day and night, *&c.* all his
works praise him. And all things declare his glory.
    Yet the tongue of men and angels is altogether unable to
speak him forth to the full.
    And as for myself,
    I must not, I cannot, I dare not say any more, but silently
adore him,   With
    O the height, the depth, the length, the breadth, how   *Rom.* 11
unsearchable! &c.
    Of him, and from him, and to him, and through him are
ALL THINGS. And he is *ALL* in *ALL*, God blessed for
evermore. *Amen*
    *Rom.*11.36. chap.9. vers.5. 1 *Cor.* 8.6. chap.11: vers.12.
2 *Cor.* 5.18. *Colos.* 1.16.17.20. *Ephes.* 1.23. and chap.4. vers.6.

III. ERROR.

That Man, or the meer Creature, is very God.

COncerning this Error.
    First I disown, detest and protest against it.
    Secondly, I affirm the contrary, *viz.*

III. ASSERTION.

That not any man, or the meer creature is very God.

For, First, the creature is mortall, I *Cor.*15.
But God is immortall, I *Tim.* 1.17. I *Tim.*6.16.
Secondly, the Creature is visible.
    But God is invisible, I *Tim.* 1.17. *John* 1. No man hath seen
God, at any time, &c.
    Thirdly, the creature is limited, and is weakness.
    But God is unlimited Almightiness.
    He is where he pleaseth, doth what he pleaseth, *Eccles.*
8.3.
    He is unlimited.

He sets up a brazen Serpent, when he pleaseth, *Numb.* 21.8,9.

And grinds it to powder, when he pleaseth, 2 Kings 18.4.

He institutes Circumcision when he pleaseth, and commands it, upon pain of Excommunication and death, &c.

Gen. 17.10,11, to the 28 verse, chap. 21.4. chap. 34.15.17. 22.24. *Exod.* 12.44.48. *Lev.* 12.3. *Josh.* 5.3.5.7. *Acts* 7.8.

All these Scriptures, I quote on purpose to shew how strictly God enjoyned Circumcision.

And what penalties were laid on them that were not obedient herein, &c.

But unlimited Almightiness dasheth that to pieces, which he made. Nuls his own Acts, Statutes, Laws, and strict Ordinances.

Nothings this great thing, Circumcision.

As it is written.

Verily Circumcision is nothing, &c. 1 *Cor.* 7.19.

And they which preached, That, up, which God (upon pain of death) once set up. Were accounted (by the holy Apostle, who was inspired with the holy Spirit) The worst of gain-sayers, unruly, vain talkers, and deceivers, *Tit.* 1.9.10.

Yea, the preaching, and practising of that, for which there were so many, so great precepts, and presidents, so large examples, and strict commands, was (at length) a horrid indignity to God, Christ, and the Gospel, &c. *Gal.* 5.2,3. *chap.* 6.12,13.

And sure there's something i'th' winde ——

Certainly the meer creature is not very God.

For the meer creature is limited, and weakness.

But God is unlimited Almightiness.

He doth what he pleaseth.

He saith, thou shalt not kill, *Exod.*20.

And yet he bids *Abraham* flay his son, &c.

He saith, Thou shalt not commit Adultery, *Exod.*20.

And fly Fornication, *Acts* 15.20.29. *chap:* 21.25. 1 *Cor.* 6:18. *Ephes.* 5.3. Col. 3.5. 1 *Thess.* 4.3.

And yet he saith to Hosea, Take a Whore - a wife of whoredomes, and get children of fornication, *Hos.* 1.2. *chap.* 3.1,2,3. Love a woman, beloved of her friend: yet an Adulteresse, &c.

Certainly the meer creature, is not very God: for the creature is limited weaknesse.

But God is unlimited Almightiness.

And doth whatsoever he pleaseth.

And who hath enjoyned him his way? Or who can say,

thou hast wrought iniquity? Or who can say to him, what dost thou? *Job* 36.23. *chap.* 9.12.

Fourthly, the meer creature is finite.

But god is infinite.   *Ergo,*

The meer creature is not very God.

I might in this argument run [*ad infinitum.*]

But let this suffice; for God is my Record, this was never my tenent, though some slanderously, others maliciously, and some through ignorance, weaknesse, and mistake, have reported it of mee.

Neither do I know any one upon the face of the Earth, that affirmeth,

That the meer creature, is very God.

IV. ERROR.

That God is in man, or in the creature onely, and no where else.

COncerning this error,

   1. I utterly dis-own, detest, and protest against it.

   2. I affirm that my holding forth the contrary, (even that sound, and Orthodoxal truth of Omni-presency) to the life: hath been one of the main stumbling blocks, whereat many have stumbled, have fallen, and have been broken.

And for which, many (who have talkt, and only talkt of Omni-presency,) have been offended at me.   But ———

   3. I assert the very truth, which is contrary to this error, (*viz.*)

IV. ASSERTION.

That God is not confined in man, or in the creature only, but is omni-present, or every where.

THat eternal, invisible, only wise God *Jehovah* [*ens entium*] the beeing of beeings, is not confined in man only, &c.

For I know that he is [*Hic, & ubique*] here, and there, and every where.

He is in the heights, in the depths, above, below.

He is in the high and lofty, that inhabits eternity.

Yet dwelleth in the lowest heart, *Isa.* 57.15.

Ps. 39.7. to the 13. Whither shall I go from thy presence? If I ascend up into Heaven, thou art there: If I make my bed in Hell, behold thou art there, &c.

Yea, the darknesse hideth not from thee: but the NIGHT

shineth as the DAY.

The DARKNESSE, and the LIGHT, are both alike to thee, &c.

He is in Heaven, Earth, Sea, Hell.

The God of the Hils, and of the Valleys also.

He is near, and afar off, &c.

He filleth all things, all places.

Can you have any more then all?

He filleth ALL in ALL, *Ephes.* 2.23.

And I am filled full, with joyous amazement; and amazing joy: that I can write no more of this subject. But shout for joy, that I know that the omnipotent *Jehovah*, is omnipresent.

[*Hallelujah, Amen.*]

For God is not confined in man, or in the creature only.

For he is in himself.

And in ALL THINGS.

For (once more) He is ALL in ALL, *Colos.*3.11.

V. ERROR.

That Cursing and Swearing, is no sin.

Concerning this thing, I shall
First declare, that for the space of 27 years, I was as free from this sin (yea, I speak as a fool) more free from it, then any that I knew, as I have already hinted in the first Assertion; whether I refer you.

But (at length) God in his infinite wisdome, (amongst many other things, for this very end, to shew to me, that at

Psal. 39

my * very best estate, I was altogether vanity.

And to take me off from mine own base bottom.

And for the destruction of the pride of my flesh.

That I might no longer glory in my self, but glory in the Lord, &c.) was pleased to turn me loose.

Job 11.12.

And being *born, a wild ass colt; and the reins being laid in my neck: I proved so indeed.

‖ Prov. 5.14.

For ‖ I was almost in all Evil.

And was infected with this plague of Swearing, &c.

But after a while, the hand of God found me out:

And sent the pangs of death to take hold on me.

*Job

*The terrours of the Almighty were set in array against me: especially for this horrid sin of Swearing: which lay upon me as a burden too heavy for me to bear. The jaws of Hell continually gaping for me.

And I concluding my self to be (as often I cryed out, I was) in a far worse case then *Cain*, or *Judas*.

And for a long season, (*a*) I lay weltring in my bloud. (a) *Ezek.* 16. My (*b*) wounds stunk, and were corrupt. (b) *Ps.*

But at length, everlasting loving kindness cast his skirts of love over me, (even (*c*) when I was cast out to the loathing of my person) when none eye pitied me, none had compassion on me. (c) *Ezek*.16.

When prayers, tears, sighs, groans, fastings, all could not cure mee.

He by his own out stretched arm, wrought wonderfully; embracing me in the arms of his tender compassion, and compassionate tenderness, saying to me, Live.

He poured both wine, and oile into my wounds, and made (*d*) the bones which he had broken, to rejoice. (d) *Psal.* 51.

And hath made me to sing.

Bless the Lord, O my soul, and all that is within me, bless his holy name.

Who forgiveth all thine iniquities, who healeth all thy diseases, &c.

I have (indeed) seen the wickedness of folly, and the foolishness of madness; and now I apply my heart to wisdome.

And therefore,

Secondly, I dis-own, detest, and protest against that error, which saith,

That Swearing and Cursing is no sin.

And in the third place, I come to the

V. ASSERTION.
That Cursing and Swearing, is a sin.

F irst, Cursing is a sin;

Because it is against that pure precept of Christ:

Bless, I say, and Curse not, *Matth*.5.44. *Luke* 6:28. *Rom*.12.14.

And that *Swearing is a Sin*:

First, I know it by woful, and most doleful experience.

I have found it so to be; with a witness.

Yea, with a vengeance, as I have afore hinted.

Furthermore, *Swearing is a sin*.

For it is a breach of that pure Commandment, which saith, *Thou shalt not take the name of the Lord thy God in vain. *Exod*. 20.

Thirdly, it is a breach of that pure precept of Christ, which saith, Swear not at all, *Matth*. 5.34.36. *ch.* 23.16.18.20,21,22.

A.C.—F

Therefore above all things, Swear not —— *Iam.* 5.

Fourthly, Swearing is a sin.

Because it pulleth down judgements upon a Land and Nation: as it is written, *Jer.* 23.10:

Because of Swearing, the Land mourns.

Because of prophane swearing, vain swearing, false swearing, for-swearing, and forc't swearing, the Land mourns.

And I mourn.

For that vengeance, and those clouds of bloud which hang over this Nation: unless the glorious beams of that bright Sunne, the Prince of peace, and God of love dispel them.

But I proceed to the sixth Error.

VI. ERROR.

That Adultery, Fornication, and Uncleannesse, is no sin.

C Oncerning this Error,
  First, I dis-own, detest, and protest against it:
Secondly, I lay down this assertion.

VI. ASSERTION.

That adultery, fornication, and uncleannesse is a sin.

F Irst, because it is a breach of that pure precept, which saith,

Thou shalt not commit adultery, *Exod.* 20.

Secondly, it is a sin against a mans own body, (as it is written) 1 *Cor.* 6.18.

He that committeth fornication, sinneth against his own body.

And I doe not remember, (that throughout the Scripture) there is the like said of any other sin besides.

Thirdly, it is against all these ensuing, wholesome, pure, precious Precepts, and Scriptures.

Acts 15:20.29. *ch.* 21.25. 1 *Cor.* 6.18. *Col.* 3.5. 1 *Thess.* 4.3.

And as for all uncleanness, let it not be once named among you. *Ephes.* 5.3.

And so I proceed to the Seventh Error, which hath some affinity with this; (*viz.*)

VII. ERROR.

That Community of Wives is lawful.

C Oncerning this Error,
First, I disown, detest, and protest against it.
Secondly, I lay down this assertion; (*viz.*)

VII. ASSERTION.	Wherein is also something hinted concerning community in the general, and concerning liberty.

That Community of wives is unlawful.

F Irst, because it is a breach of that pure Precept.
1 *Cor.* 7.2. Let every man have his own wife, and every woman her own husband.

Secondly, this tenent, is a corrupt opinion, that Christ hates; which is briefly hinted in that of *Revel.* 2.6.

This thou hast, that thou hatest the deeds of the *Nicolaitans*, which I also hate.   I will add,

Thirdly, that it is destructive to the dearest, and nearest relations, and the occasion of multitudes of miseries and perplexities.

Fourthly, it is destructive to the [*bene esse*] —— Well-beeing of a Common-wealth.

And here I think good to give a hint of community in the general, because I understand, I have been by some traduced, and by others mistaken, concerning it.

I shall only here say,

That there is something (by some) contended for, in the name of community: which may prove meerly pernicious, and exceedingly destructive in several respects.

But for mine own part,

I shall [*ex animo*] in the presence of God, declare to the whole world, and here recite what I have formerly written, in my Remonstrance ——   Thus,

As for community, I own none but that Apostolical, saint-like community, spoken of in the Scriptures.

So far I either do, or should own community, that if flesh of my flesh, be ready to perish; I either will, or should call nothing that I have, mine own.

If I have bread, it shall, or should be his, else my religion is in vain. I am for dealing bread to the hungry, for cloathing the naked, for the breaking of every yoak, for the letting of the oppressed go free. I am, or should be as my heavenly Father, who is kind to all, loving to all, even to the ungodly, &c. *Mat.* 6.

I can (through grace) pity those that are objects of my compassion, and out of poverty and penury relieve those that are in want.   Yet,

Know all men by these presents, that I am utterly against that community which is sinful, or destructive to soul or body, or the well-beeing of a Common-wealth.

And as for liberty,

I do from my heart detest, and protest against all sinfull liberty, or that is destructive to soul or body; or the [*bene esse*] the well-beeing of a Common-wealth.

Rom. 8.   I own none other, long for none other, but that* glorious liberty of the sons of God:

Which God will hasten in its time.

[Conclusion.]

Till then, though I have been (through my over-much zeal, and through the weakness and mistake of others, an offence to many:

Cor. 10.32,33.   Yet (through grace) I will* give no offence for the future, either to Jew or Gentile, or to the Church of God.

And resolve (by the grace of God) to live at peace with all men.

And I give the world to understand, that those that are godly, sincere, and conscientious in their waies: (let them bee where they will) I own them, love them: they are the

Rom. 14.2.   very joy of my soul. I will neither be offended* at my weak brother, which eateth hearbs. Nor judge my strong brother, which eateth meat.

*Rom.*14.   Neither will I judge my brother that* observeth a DAY: if to the Lord he observeth it.

Nor judge him that observeth not a day: if to the Lord he observeth it not.

To the Lord of the Conscience,

And to the Lord of ALL,

Even to the Lord, I leave you all,

And in the Lord, I love you all.

And in him,

Farewell. AMEN.

A Preamble to the ensuing
PROPOSALS,
and ANSWERS

*Since the finishing of my former —— this ensuing Letter, with
the several Proposals therein contained, were sent to me by the
Reverend M.Dury, which with my full and faithful Answer
thereunto, may be aptly added as a second part to the former Tract.*

*And to winde up all, it is thought expedient that my last Letter,
(to my worthily respected and faithful friend) concerning this
businesse, &c*
        Be annexed as a Conclusion of All ——

M. *Coppe,*

ALthough we all who conferred with you yesterday,
came with some fore-stalment against you (as by our
Discourses you might well perceive) yet when we parted
from you, I found, as in my self, so in all the rest, that your
Declarations to us had left an impression in us, that you
were ingenuously open in what you then said; and that we
had the cause to believe that you were really sensible of, and
truly penitent for that which you had formerly done: which
being so, you ought conscientiously to bethink your self,
how to give satisfaction unto the world of the truth of your
conversion. Let me therefore give you an opportunity, to
testifie unto all, that which was declared unto us, and did
seem a true evidence of your repentance: if then you would
as in the fear of God by way of Letter to some of us, lay open
your sense concerning the things which I shall now lay
before you; you would do your self much right, in our
opinion who conferred with you, and it will bee an
advantage towards the accomplishment of your desires as
God may direct us to improve it.

First, then, although the tediousness, and other inconveniences of your imprisonment, may be lawful and natural
motives to you to desire a releasement; yet it will bee
expedient for your own comfort, to make it appear before
God to your own conscience, that you dissemble not your
repentance to flatter him with your lips, (for God cannot be
deceived) and before men, whose eyes are upon you, that
you make not a fair profession of being effectually converted
only to gain your liberty; that then as a Sow, you may return
again to wallow in the mire: I say, it will be very expedient,
that you clear up these things, both to your self, and to other

men; for as you ought to suspect your self, so others will be ready to suspect you of this.

Secondly, you will do well to speak fully and plainly your sense of things whereof I discoursed with you, after that you had opened your self in the things taken notice of by us, in your Preface, *viz.*

Concerning Sin; What you understand it to be? Whether any thing be otherwise a sin, then as men imagine it to themselves to bee so? Whether men please God as well when they sinne, as when they sinne not? And whether to act most sinne, bee the nearest way to perfection? And what you think of these Tenets; and whether the Fiery Flying Roll, doth not insinuate them to be Truths, and dispose men to receive them as such?

Concerning the Law of God declare your sense of it; as whether it is not a rule to all men of their life in thoughts, words, and deeds? where the infallible testimony thereof is to be found, where unto all men must appeal and submit; and whether there be else where any truth of God to be believed besides that which is witnessed by every mans spirit unto himself?

Concerning God and the souls of men, what you think of him? and whether he hath not a being before, and out of all creatures in himself from eternity? what difference there is between the nature of mens souls, and his being? and in what sense we are said to partake of the Divine nature. 2. *Pet.* 1.4.

Concerning the resurrection of the body, and the last judgement, what you believe thereof? and whether you think these things to be past already, as to any men living on earth, yea or no.

The third thing which I have to offer unto you, is the consideration of the circumstances whereby your sins are highly aggravated, and for which you should use means to make your repentance the more remarkable.

First, in respect of your own person; for you have been a preacher, and a leading man; now a sin in such a person is more dishonourable to God, and to the holy profession, then in other men; therefore their repentance ought to be more remarkebly satisfactory then other mens repentance.

Secondly, in respect of the publick and noted manner of your failings, you ought proportionably to make your humiliation the more publick and notable.

Thirdly, in respect of the grievousness, and hainousness of the actions in themselves, they being of a very deep dye; you ought to wipe them away with the greater contrition before God; and to evidence your turning from them with the greater abhorrency thereof before men; and with the more care of giving a ful assurance to the State, that you shall never return thereunto again.

Fourthly, in respect of the hurt which your Doctrine and perswasion, or example hath done to the souls of other men; whereof som you have led into the waie of perdition, who perhaps will never be reclaimd; & others you have so scandaliz'd that the way of truth is evil spoken of by them: all which should lie heavily upon your spirit all your days; that from henceforth you should strive to make so much the more amends, by being more examplary in holiness, then ever you have been in dissoluteness.

If you will express your thoughts concerning these things, and pray to God to direct you both in thinking and expressing you will do that which becometh your in-genuitie; and add to the satisfaction which was wanting in your former discourse, and is now expected to be improved for your good, by

your willing servant in
Christ, John Dury.

June 23. 1651.

For his much honoured Friend Mr Dury

SIR,

I Have joyfully and thankfully received yours, with your wholsom advise therein contained.

And I give you to understand,
      That
My desires jump with your requirings, and in the laying open of my sense, concerning the things which you lay before me.

And first concerning the nature and grounds of my desires, in reference to my releasement, *&c.*

And therein —— first Negatively:

I do not desire or seek after my Liberty, to this end, That I might return again, and wallow in the mire.

For I had rather die a thousand deaths, then so do: or desire so to do.

Neither do I, or did I dissemble my repentance, or flatter God with my lips.

For all those fair professions, sparkling through my Book,

and those which (so solemnly in the presence of God, and before you with seriousness, and sorrow of heart, and tears in mine eyes,) I made, came from the bottom of my soul; cordially, fervently, and compunctionately: as the searcher of the heart knows, my conscience also bearing me witness.

And although (as you say, and I know) the tediousness, and several other inconveniences of mine imprisonment may be, and are lawful and natural motives to me, to desire a releasment.

Yet I say, and give you to understand, (and that from the bottom of my heart) these are not the main motives ──

But the prime, chief, and principal, is

That I might be in a better way, place, posture, and capacity to glorifie God, then I possibly can be in here.

For how can I sing the songs of my God in a strange land, &c.

I do in the presence of God (even from my soul) with grief, gasp, and cordially, and feelingly breath out those groans.

Wo is me, that I am constrained to sojurn in Mesech, and to inhabit in the tents of Kedar, &c.

Truly, Sir,

I have a long, long while eaten* Grass with Oxen.

Verbum sat ──

These, and the like ── are the prime grounds of my groaning under the burden of my imprisonment: which next to my sins is one of the heaviest, &c.

And so I come to your other Proposals.

And first, to the first, which runs thus:

*Vid. Preface to my last book, p.7

Prop. I. *What do you understand sin to be?*

Answ. In general, I understand sin, (which is my most unsupportable burden) to be the transgression of THE Law.

Against which we (in innumerable wayes) transgress; in thoughts, words, deeds; in omissions, commissions, ignorance, weakness, and presumption, &c.

But to your second, *viz.*

Prop. II. *Whether any thing be otherwise a sin, then as men imagine it to themselves to be?*

Answ. I answer, That sin, is sin in it self, yea, (as the Apostle saith)† exceeding sinful.

†Rom.

Even every breach, (yea, the least breach) of THE Law, is sin. Whether men imagine it to themselves so to be, or no.

For instance:

Adultery is a sin, whether men imagine it to be so, or no.

Even adultery – of all sorts; corporal, or spiritual; which

the whole Land, and every mans heart (even the heart of the purest and strictest) is brim full of; if they could see it.

But ALL adulterers (I say) of all sorts, whether corporal, or spiritual: and S. *James* hist adulterers, and adulteresses, are sinners, do sin, whether they imagine it so, or no. †*James* 4.1: *to the 6. vers.*

Yea,* heart adultery, and eye adultery, lust in both, in either is sin, sin with a witness. *Mat.* 5.28. *Whereof those are greatly guilty that cry out of adultery & uncleaness in others, &c.

Whether men imagin it to be so or no.

But I know it so to be: and (with a witness) have found it so to be:

And I still remember, and shall never forget that I heard a reverend Divine (when I was about sixteen years old) affirm, That heart-adultery, *&c.* was worse then the act of adulterie, *&c.* It being the father and spirit of adulterie.

As also (many times) reaching such objects which were (at that time——) free from the like lust, *&c.*

I do not say that I am of his opinion.

But sure I am, this express hath (hundreds of times) wounded me to the very heart; and hath (for many years) stuck as a dagger in my soul; and hath cost me hot waters, even many, many showrs of tears; and innumerable sighs and groans, *&c.*

And let him that is without sin (in this particular) cast the first stone at adulterers, and adulteresses.

And (for my part, as I have been cut and wounded, wounded to the heart for this: so will I throw stones (as fast as I can drive) at ADULTERY, at all sorts of adultery: in my self, and others, which I know to be sin, and sin of a deep dye: Yea, a crimson crime, whether men imagine it to be so or no.

And so is swearing and cursing, *&c.* a sin, as I have* to my great grief, and sore smart found it to be: and I once more proclaim it so to be.

*Vid. truth triumphing over error, &c. Pag.27.

Whether men imagine it to be so or no.

And so is drunkness of all sorts (and there are various sorts thereof) a sin.

Whether men imagine it to be so or no.

And theft of all sorts (and there are several sorts thereof) a sin.

Whether men imagine it to be so or no.

And murther of all sorts (and there are several sorts thereof, and several sorts of Murtherers) a sin.

Whether men imagine it to be so or no.

And there are thousands of Drunkards, thieves and murtherers (of several sorts) who stroak themselves on the head, and say, I thank God, I am not as this drunkard, thief, or as this murtherer, *&c.*

And yet go away no more justified then the worst of Publicans and sinners.

But for my part I will not justifie any of these in my self, or in others.

For once more, I say, and know, that drunkenness of all sorts: theft of all sorts, and murther of all sorts, is a sin.

Whether men imagine it to be so, or no.

*Jam. 2. And so is pride, covetousness, hypocrisie, oppression, Tyranny, cruelty, unmercifulnesse, *despising the poor and needy, who are in vile raiment, &c.

A sin.

Whether men imagine it to be so or no.

And so is doing unto others, as we would not be done unto our selves, &c.

A sin.

Whether men imagine it to be so or no.

And the laying of Nets, Traps, and Snares for the feet of our neighbours, is a sin.

Whether men imagine it to be so or no.

And so is the not undoing of heavy burthens, the not letting the oppressed go free: the not breaking every yoak, and the not dealing of bread to the hungry, &c. and the hiding our selves from our own flesh, &c.

A sin.

Whether men imagine it to be so or no.

And let this suffice for answer to your second *Proposal*, Wherein I affirm,

That sin is sin whether men imagine it to be so or no.

And as for the FIERY FLYING ROLL,

I disclaim, declaim, and protest against it which doth (to use your own apt expression) *insinuate the contrary.*

Also I once more, disclaim, declaim, and protest against all other Errors, and blasphemous opinions therein insinuated, &c.

As my large, free, cordial professions to you, and what I have now written on this point, and that which here followeth.

As also the assertion of so many truths, in my former writings, together with those many protestations against mine own errors, as also against others that I have not been tackt or tainted with, do clearly demonstrate to all ingenuous, and unprejudiced spirits.

Even to all, unless to those that will be satisfied with nothing; but rejoyce to add afflictions to my bonds, and to spit out their inveterate and secret malice against me, &c.

But to the Lord I leave them. And to him I refer my cause who Registers my groans, and hears the sighing of the

90

prisoners.

And knows the sincerity of my heart which he hath given me;

And I proceed to the rest of your Proposals.

Which (I humbly conceive) might have been more aptly proferrd to the authors of such *Assertions*, from whence your proposals have their rise, *&c.* then to me who am not the father of them nor did ever own them, &c.

And for my part I am indisposed to meddle with other mens matters.

And am also filled with various perplexities, griefs, and languishments, & so compassed about with so many inconveniencies with weaknesse of my body, and various distempers both of body and minde; and altogether wanting all manner of accomodations: being also sorely put to it for place —— and opportunity.

That I am very unfit for these things.

However (so well as I can) I proceed to your 3, and 4, Proposals, *viz.*

III. and } Propos. *Whether men please God as well when*
IV. *they sin, as when they sin not?*

And,

Whether to act most sin, be the nearest way
to perfection?

Answ. I answer, That I disown, detest, and protest against this opinion, as erronous and blasphemous.

And contrary to the whole tenure of Scripture:

As also contrary to mine own experience.

For I am perswaded,

That never any man hath lien more under the wrath and heavy displeasure of God for sin, then I have done.

And as for the Scriptures, they affirm,

That when God saw that the wickedness of man was great upon the earth: and that every imagination of the thoughts of his heart, was only *Evil* continually: it repented the Lord that he had made man on the earth, and it grieved him at his heart, and that he was sore displeased thereat —— he said,——

I will destroy man whom I have created, both man and beast, *&c. Gen.* 6.5,6,7.11,12,13.

The time would fail to summ up all the Scriptures to this purpose. *&c.*

Neither can I at this time in this place, be in a capacity to do it.

But I go on.

When Israel, Gods peculiar (seperated people) had

sinned, *Num* 14.

The Lord said, how long will this people provoke me? I will smite them with the pestilence, *&c:* vers. 11,12.

And again how long shal I bear with this evil congregation? as truly as I live your Carcasses shall fall in the wildernesse, *&c.* vers. 27,28,29.

Again, they ceased not from their own doings, but have transgressed, *&c.*

And the anger of the Lord was hot against Israel, *&c. Judg.* 2:19. to the end of the chap.

And Chap. 3.7,8,9,10,11,12. 1 *King.* 11. from vers. to the 12.

These, and 100 more —— yea, the whole current of the Scripture holds forth what I affirm, and maintain.

That God is highly displeased with men for sin, *&c.*

And that to act sin is the highest way to perfection, is a thing I never heard started before; neither did I ever hear of any that held it.

It is a Tenet so simply and sinfully absurd, That I abhor it.

And therefore I utterly disown it, detest it, and protest against it as so.

And I know and affirm, That the more sinful any one is, the more imperfect —— and divellish. For [*he that committeth sin, is of the Divel,* &c.] according to the Scripture, and God who is perfect sinneth not: and is displeased with them that do sin.

And I come to your fift *Proposal,* viz.

V. Propos. *What is my sense of the Law of God.* —— *&c.*

Answ. In answer hereunto,

Rom. 2. First, I declare and affirm the Law to be* holy, and just, and good, *&c.*

Secondly, That is a rule to all men of their lives, in thoughts, words, and deeds, *&c.*

And that the infallible testimony thereof is to be found in the word of God, whereunto all men must appeal and submit: and which they must believe: neither are they to adhere to any thing that is without, or contrary to the word, *&c.*

* 2 *Tim.* 3.15,16. *And that the holy Scriptures are able to make —— wise unto salvation, through faith which is in C.Jesus, *&c.*

And all Scripture is given by inspiration of God, and is profitable, *&c.*

And so I come to your 6. *Proposal,* viz.

VI. Propos. *What I think of God, and the souls of men,* &c.

Answ. I answer,

Concerning God (of whom I have, and doe write, with fear and trembling, &c.) I have spoken at large, in several particulars, in several Chapters, or under several Heads, in my Manuscript, called, *Truth asserted*, &c. *Assertion* 2,3,4. from P.8. to the 11.

To all which I shall add this affirmative to your (now) *Quere*, viz.

That God hath a being before, and out of all creatures, in himself, from eternity.

And as for the difference between the nature of mens souls, and his being.

I believe,

That he hath his being in himself.

And men have their souls from him, *&c*

And concerning our partaking of the Divine nature, &c.

This is my sense,

That we are partakers of the Divine nature, through our Mystical, and Spiritual Filiation, *&c*.

For as the son of man partakes of his fathers nature, so the sons of God (in a glorious spiritual, and unspeakable manner) partake of his nature.

As it is written,* Because we are sons, therefore hath he given us his spirit, *&c*.   *Rom. Galat.

And the love of God is shed abroad in our hearts, *&c*.

We are partakers of the Divine nature.

Through that glorious, Mystical, unfathomable, Spiritual union which we have with Christ, and his in-dwelling in us, *&c*:

And concerning this union, and in-dwelling: so much is throughout the Scripture:

First, Typified.

Secondly, Metaphoriz'd.

Thirdly, Alegoriz'd.

Fourthly, Prophesied.

Fifthly, Promised, [*That it should be made manifest.*]

Sixtly, In plain Scripture tearms expressed.

And

Seventhly, Joyful and gloriously experienced.

This glorious Mystery (I say) which hath been* hid from ages, and from generations, *&c*.   *Colos. 1.26.27.

Is held forth (in the Scriptures of truth) in Types, Allegories, Metaphors, Prophecies, promises in plain tearms, and all this confirmed by joyful experience.

And now being* he that sanctifieth, and they that are sanctified are —— one, and he is not ashamed to call them brethren.   *Joh. 6. Heb.2.

And being he is* in them, —— dwels in them. *&c, Joh. 16.*

93

Col. 1.26,27. 2 Cor. 6.16.

And being in him dwels ALL the fulness of the God-head bodily —— *&c.*

Of his fulness we all receive, *Joh. 1. Colos.*

Wherefore I say, of and from, and through him —— though mystical, spiritual, filiation, fraternity, unity, and in-dwelling. *We are partakers of the Divine nature.*

And so I come to your seventh Proposal, *viz.*

VII. Propos. *What I think of the resurrection of the body, &c.*
And the last judgement, &c.

Answ. To this I answer,

First, That I am no *Saduce*, and am as unwilling to be a *Pharisee.*

Secondly, concerning these points: I have never discoursed, preached, or writ any thing.

Thirdly, I believe the resurrection of the body, *&c.*

According to the Scriptures and especially —— that of 1*Cor.* 15.35 to the 54.

And concerning the great day of Judgement;
I believe,

That the dead, both small and great, shall stand before God the Judge of all, and the Books shall be opened, and the dead shall be judged out of those things which are written in the Books, according to their works, *Rev.* 20.12.

Neither do I think these things to be past already as to any man living on Earth. But the contrary.

And as for those things which you offer to me, concerning the
circumstances whereby my sins are aggravated, &c.

I have took them into my sad and serious consideration.

And those —— with divers others —— have been set home upon my spirit by the hand of God, &c.

And as for my repentance, and turning from them; and for the satisfaction of all, &c. I doe not desire that what I have spoken, and to that purpose written, may be put under a bushel: or confined in a corner, but that it might fly abroad, to that end, &c.

And furthermore, in what way and places soever divine providence shall dispose of me, I shal not cease to publish it, and what God hath wrought in me.

And as for my giving assurance to the State —— which you speak of

I neither have assuarance of my self; nor can I have it from man.

But my assuarance is in God: in whom I have hope, and full affiance, That (through his grace) I shall never return thereto again.

As I have humbly, sincerely, and cordially (both in my humble Petition to them, and in several other places of my writing) exprest.

And that my future deportment in all things, shall make amends for what hath been by-past, &c.

And thus have I faithfully, sincerely, (and as I conceive) fully fulfilled mine own desires, and answered your requirings, in adding to what I have formerly written, and to all my large professions, and protestations, &c.

This Answer to your several *Proposals*, &c.

All which, I hope, (according to your promises ——) will be improved for my good:

For which I pray, and hope, &c: And which also I humbly expect from you.

Hoping (that according to your profession, and those good thoughts I have of you) you will look upon me, upon my expressions, and writings; and upon my condition (which in several respects, is very sad) as your own.

——*Considering also your self* ——

That I may finde by experience, that the golden Law of all true Righteousness —— and love, is written in your heart.

The tenure whereof runs thus:

Whatsoever you would that men should do unto [and for] you,
Even so do you unto [And FOR] them.
For this is the LAW, and the Prophets.

And I am

Honoured SIR,

Newgate, June 28.1651

Your humble and faithful
servant
in THE LORD,

ABIEZER COPPE.

For his much Honoured friend, Mr. Marchamont Nedham.

M. Nedham!
My humble service, sincere respects, and hearty commendations to you presented, &c.

A Lthough I have been (by sickness, weakness, and various distempers of body and mind) impeded, &c.

Yet I have at length finished these.

And now I present them to you.

As for my former Writings, which you and the other Gentlemen lately received; I cannot question, but that I have (now) fully fulfilled your desires, and requirings therein.

By deleating what might prove offensive to any.

By altering, correcting, and amending other things. And

By explicating some other things that might appear dubious, or difficult.

And herein I have not omitted the least clause ———

Wherefore I cannot question but that it may now pass:

And as for M. *Duries* ———

I have faithfully, sincerely, (and as I conceive) fully, (and I hope, satisfactorily) answered his Letter, and those various Proposals therein contained, &c.

And concerning your last ——— *About the Fiery Flying Roll,* &c.

——— Thus:

Although (in the former Copy of my Book, *Page 5,6.*) I spoke concerning the blasphemous opinions which it insinuated only by way of question and supposition, &c. yet now doe I there, and more at large elsewhere,

First, positively acknowledge, that it doth so ———

As you may see there, and more at large, in my answer to M. *Dury.*

And, Secondly, there is not any one, from the greatest to the least error, therein insinuated, which I do not (both cordially, and zealously) declaim and protest against, &c.

And, Thirdly, I have faithfully (and I humbly conceive) fully, asserted Truths: contrary to every one of the Errors therein insinuated, and to divers other Errors which I have not been (in the least degree) takct or tainted withal, &c.

Which I hope may give full satisfaction. I having (according to your advise) proceeded therein roundly, freely, and fully.

And (now) my humble request to you is,

That you would please to prosecute your good enterprise

—— in my behalf, &c.
        Truly, Sir,
Hope deferred, maketh the heart sick.

And my languishing expectations will be more grievous to me, then my tedious imprisonment: unless they are satisfied, &c.

These, and my sad condition (which is so indeed in several respects) I make bold to present to your Christian, charitable consideration.

Relying on your sweetness, and goodness, for a continuation of your former, and undeserved favours.

And I shall joyfully subscribe my self,

                                        SIR

NEWGATE, June 28. 1651.

Your faithful servant, and
*   a well-wisher*
to you and you vertues.

        ABIEZER COPPE.

FINIS.

DIVINE FIRE-WORKS

OR,

Some Sparkles from the Spirit of BURNING in
this dead Letter.
HINTING
What the Almighty Emanuel is doing in these
WIPPING Times.
AND
In this HIS day which burns as an OVEN.

IN *ABHIAM.*

Can any good come out of ————— *? Come and See.*

T He LYON, who a long time sleeped,
Is (by the *Consuming* Fire) out of his Den fired.
Being rouzed,
He roared,
The Beasts of the Forrest trembled.
Were any of the children frighted?
Have any of them stumbled?
Sure I am the Heathen raged.
Have any of the PEOPLE (also) a vain thing imagined?

**This was the
Lord knows where
the 29th of the last
mon. An. BLVI &
besides spectators
and auditors,*

The Hell Hounds yelled. By CRAVC-VR *witnessed.*
The Dogs with open mouth gaped, and greatly barked.
At length
The men of *Sodom* were (strangely) with blindness smitten.
The Dogs mouths which were so wide open, were (with a pure and heavenly cunning) stopped:
They also fawned, and their tails wagged, &c.
It's the earnest of good things to come.
And thus saith our Almighty Emanuel,
My wayes are unsearchable, and my Iudgements past finding out, &c.
O the heights! and depths! and lengths! and breadths! how unsearchable? &c.
The rest is torn out,

Yet it's written
From
My joyous Fiery-fornace, where I am in the Spirit on the LORDS DAY.
Which burns as an Oven,
And where I am joyfully dwelling
With everlasting *Burnings.*
This first day of the $\left\{\begin{array}{l} BLVI. \\ BLVII. \end{array}\right.$ A.B.
New Year,
London printed in the beginning of the year, BLVII.
Felt, heard, and understood, manifested and
Revealed at the end of —— An. —— BLVI.
Let none but Angels sing this round,
The end hath the *beginning* found.
And what and if one risen from the dead, &c.
And what and if a sleepy Lyon out of his Den fired, &c.
Should tell you the truth? could ye in any wise believe?
Hoc accidit dum vile fuit

CHAP. II.

The sight, reception, and enjoyment of the TRUE BLV
(which far surpasseth the Philosophers Stone, &c.
Hinted at.
—— *Hoc accidet dum vile fui*
For wo is me, I am undone, I have seen the Lord the King.
I am undone. I am a fool.

Suffer fools gladly; if you may, if you can.
If I am a fool, it is for your sakes.
I am besides my self; and if I am ——— it is to God
I am not ——— for God hath took me.
I am undone, yet gloriously and joyfully undone.
I have seen the Lord. THE King;
  Who appeared unto me
On [*Innocents Day*] the 28 of the last moneth.
He spake to me and with me, (as a friend speaketh to
his friend) of things unspeakable and unutterable.

By* night (on my bed also) he whom my soul loveth, set
before mine eye, both mental and corporal.
                    BLV
Exceeding glorious, most transparent and most transplendent.
  And what I am now about (with fear & trembling, as
also with high rejoycing) I can present to you, no more,
no otherwise, then as part of the black, dark shadow of
a man, against a sun shine wall, &c.
  At this strange, glorious, and unexpected sight,
  The Spirit of Burning (by which the filth of the
daughter of Sion is purged) did so surround me, and took
such real possession of me,
  That it not onely waxed hot within me;
  But also (on a sudden) set my body on such a flame;
that (at a distance) it would warm the stander by, as if
they were warming their hands at a burning fire, &c.
  Then was I raised to sit up in my bed (in my shirt)
smoaking like a furnace.
  And with glorious holy fear and trembling, I bowed the
Knees of my soul; as also my body
  With all awful reverence before the dreadful, (yet to his
friends) the glorious presence of the God of *Abraham*, the
God of *Isaac*, the God of *Jacob*.
  With my hands wringing, the Spirit groaning,
        And at length saying,
I beseech thee, I beseech thee, I beseech thee
                Tell me what is this?
  Then HE spake;
  Whose voice once shook the earth; But now not onely
the earth, but the heavens also   Saying,
Fear not, it is I BLVI.
  Whereupon the Spirit within me (with exceeding joy)
exceedingly groaned, & with a loud voice, out sounded
      O the BLV! O the BLV! O the BLV!
And the worm, and no man said, what BLV;
Lord

He, as a loving Father, gave me (as it were) a box 'ith' ear,
saying,

Dost not remember, when thou was't a School boy,
thou heard'st this saying,

TRUE BLV wil never stain, will never fail,

White is the signal of Innocency. BLV, of Truth ——

And I that am incomprehensible, without colour,
invisible,

Yet in (an unfathomable sense) *as visible,   *Heb*.11.27

And as I may, can, & wil so say;

I both have, can, wil, & do appear in my COULOURS, at
my pleasure.

The White —— as Innocency, the BLV —— as trueth.

TRUE BLVI, True BLVI I AM.

And though I am in heaven, earth, & hel, &c.

Yet earth, hel & heaven, yea the heaven of heavens is not
able to contain me, &c.

Now have I in an unspeakable eminent way bowed the
heavens, & am come down upon the earth. And will
shew my self,

As in my Coulors, —— &c.

Whereupon he drew a sharp two edged flaming
sword, &c.

(Another manner of Sword then that hee wore on Mount
Sina)

Saying,

Bear thou the typical testimony thereof.

And in a dark, low, beggarly shadow, wear BLV,

With this Superscription,

TRUE BLV I will never fail,

TRUTH is great, and will prevail.

And (nor conferring with flesh and blood) I was
obedient to the heavenly commandment.

Whereupon with an exceeding holy fear and trembling,
filled brim-ful [also] of joy and rejoycing,

I bowed down both soul and body, before the God of
Abraham, Isaac, and *Jacob*.

And the Spirit within me sounded forth, O eternal
spirit of TRUTH, which wil never fail.

What am I, a worm, and no man? ——

— *A* Nazarite (By the Lord of Hosts, which dwelleth in
Mount Sion) made blacker then a cole—

—— Not known in the streets ——

Known at home Only.

Fear thou not, I am thine, & I am with thee and a wal
of fire round about thee.

I will also tell thee what I am doing in

These whipping Times,
And in this my Day
Which burns as an *OVEN.*
Hark!

---

*Chap.*III
What the Lord *is doing these whipping Times? &c.*

Hark!
The noise of a whip, on top of the Mountains,
Whip and burn, whip and burn, whip & burn,
I, THE consuming fire in An.BL*V*II ——
have bowed the heavens, & am come down,
I am come to baptize with the Holy Ghost, and with *Fire.

some have felt it with a witness.

My Fan is in my hand, and I will *throughly purge* my *Floor,*&c. But,
The chaff I will burn up, with unquenchable Fire.
O chaff, chaff, hear the Word of the Lord.
To the unquenchable fire thou must, it is thy doom.

It's a whipping Time. The day burns as an Oven.
Wherein (II) all the proud, and all that do wickedly shall be stubble. And the day that cometh, and [NOW is] shall BURN them up.
It shal leave them neither root nor branch.
Mal.4.1. Learn what that meaneth,
Whom it hitteth, it hitteth.
It's a whipping time.

And he that a TRUTH, and no lye, hath bowed the heavens, and is come down.
(III) TO whip the Thieves out of his own *Temple. And amongst all the rabble that are there, he wil whip out that old thief, that foul & unclean spirit that saith, Stand back, I am holier then thou, &c.

† *Ye are the Temple of the living God, as God hath said,* I *will dwell in them, &c.* ICor. 6. 2 Cor.6 15.

That Thief also shall not scape his Lash, who saith, L*o here, or to shere,* &c,
These are whipping time; and
The day *Burns* as an Oven.

And thus saith my God,
Who (to my exceeding, exceeding joy) is a consuming Fiie, I have bowed the heavens, and am come down.

(IV) To cry every mans work so as by *Fire*; and this consuming fire shall enter into the marrow and the bones, and search the heart and the veins:

*A*nd shall go on and do its work, as it hath begun:

And turn the IN-side outwards.

To the eternal fame of some; and to the everlasting shame of others.

Let the later expect what is upon them coming with a vengeance.

The day burns like an Oven.

For (V) He hath bowed the Heavens and is coming down in flaming Fire,

To render vengeance to those that know him not; especially to those who talk much of him, yet call him, *Beelzebub, &c. &c. &c.*

These are whipping times.

For [VI) he hath bowed the heavens, and
is come down to whip

These froward foolish children who call their Father Rogue, if he appear in any other garb then what they have usually seen in him, &c.

And he will never give over whipping them, till they give over saying to him, What dost thou?

Till they give over Injoyning him his way, &c.

*A*nd their daring to be so arrogantly foolish, as

To JUDGE the things THEY know not ——

He that hath an ear to hear let him hear.

And AL shall feel
It is a whipping time.

For (VII) He hath bowed the Heavens,
and is come down to whip and burn,
whip and burn. ——

None shall escape his lash,

No not his dearly beloved Daughter of *Sion*.

Among many other things he will soundly scourge her for her haughtinesses, and outstretched-neckedness.

For holding her neck so high.

For her cursed Scorn, Hellish Pride and niceness.

For not remembring her Sister *Sodom* in the day of her pride, &c.

And the roaring ramping Lyon, with the sharp two-edged Sword, wil run her through and through.

And with unquenchable fire
Will burn up the bravery of their tinkling Ornaments.
The bracelets, &c. The changeable Suits of apparel, &c.
The Glasses, and fine Linnen. The Hoods and the
Vails, &c.

And instead of sweet smelling there shall be a stink;
and BURNING instead of Beauty.

And because she turneth away her eyes from her own
flesh, yea, and denies her own Spirit and Life;

Yea, her Father that begot her; and

Her eldest Brother, the Heir of all,

For this her haughtiness, and stretched-neckedness,
she shall not onely be whipt, but also the crown of the
head of the Daughter of *Sion* shall be smitten with a *Scab*.
And

The Lord wil discover her SECRET parts.

And this shall be done to the green Tree.

And if this be done to the green Tree,

[VII] What shall be done to the Dry Tree?

At present I will not tell them.

They shall feel with a witness, &c.

And Ile only here insert a Prophecie, which sparkled
forth from the Spirit of Prophecy, before these whipping
times were thought on or expected.

The Prophecy.

Sith that their wayes they do not mend,

Ile finde a Whip to scourge them by;

And with my Rod Ile make them bend,

and so divide them suddainly,

This is but the beginning of sorrows.

And this that is now (in this dead Letter hinted) is but
the bare contents of some of those many things which the
consuming fire is about to do these whipping times; and
in this day which BURNS as an Oven; and where in
triumphs and joy I now live.

You shall have it more at large one way or other, one
time or other.

The End

Is not yet.

London, Printed for the Author,

Jan. 20. An.   { BLVI
                   BLVII.

Written *Jan*. I & 3. *An*.   {   56.
                                  57.

True BLVI will never fail;
TRUTH is great, & will prevail.

A
Character of a true Christian.

Written by *Abiezar Copp*,   The Tune is, *The Fair Nimphs*.

Love.

A Christian true doth love
　　his Father that's above,
　　His Brother that's below.
　　his Friends, and eak his
Foe,
The Rich, the Poor, the great, the
small,
the Strong, the Weak, he loveth
all.

Self-denyal.

He still denyes himself,
　　not greedily gripes for Pelf,
Doth nether pole nor pill,
　　his Chests or Barns to fill,
His Neighbours Good, not Goods,
doth seek,
　　he's honest, harmless, loving,
meek.

Humility.

Not pust in mind is he:
　　all those of low degreee,
Do never taste his Scorn,
　　the Base, the Vile, Forlorn:
He's bounteous, curteous, loving
and kind,
　　to all he bears a gentle mind.

Stability.

He still at home doth keep,
　　and his own door doth sweep;
Doth not debase his mind,

in seeking Faults to find:
He picks no hole in Neighbours
Coat,
   nor strives in's Ey to finde a
Mote.

Forbearance.

His Lamb-like spirit doth bear,
   he doth not fight nor tear,
Nor flounce, nor fling, nor fume,
   but Meekness doth perfume
His Soul, when he is injured,
   captivity is captive led.

Mercy.

His burning Bowels yern,
   from thence his Eye doth learn,
To 'still some oyl of Right
   into the wretched Weight.
His hand is fired by his heart,
   his substance to the poor to
impart.

Charity.

His Charity is not small,
   it doth extend to all,
The bad and eke the good:
   not like the formal Mode,
Who none but their own sect
endure,
   this is from the Fountain pure.

Wisdom.

He wisely walks to all
   and to prevent a Fall,
He looks before he leaps:
   a narrow Watch he keeps,
When to speak, he well doth see,
   and when silent he's to be.

Peace.

His Principle is Peace,
   in him all Wars do cease,
The sword and Gown may stand,
   both distant from his Land,
He is endear'd to great and small,
   he lives in Love and Peace with all.

Obedience.

He marcheth in the Van,
   to each Decree of man,
For God's sake he subjects,
   to all he yields respects,
The Prince of Peace doth Peace impart,
   he hates all Plots with all his heart.

Freedom.

The Sun hath made him Free
   from *AEgypts* Slavery,
From daily Brick and Task,
   he needs no religious Mask,
Through Christ he all things doth and can,
   he's wholy the Lords free man.

Patience.

He bravely bears the Cross,
   and sits down by the loss,
When *Sabeans* on him fall,
   and *Caldees* take his all
Not these nor those, but God in Heav'n,
   he saith, Hath taken as well as giv'n.

Content.

Soul-killing Discontent,
  whereby pure life is spent,
And marrow melts away,
  with him it cannot stay:
His Soul in Patience doth posses,
  for, Evil and Good the Lord
doth bless.

Resignation.

For wholly he's resigned
  unto the Unconfin'd,
God's pleasure is his Law,
  of that he stands in aw.
When Self is swept away and
gone,
  he sayes and lives, *God's Will be
done.*

London, Printed by *T.D.* sold by *La: Curtiss.* 1680

Appendix: Die Veneris, I Februarii, 1649

Die Veneris, 1 Februarii, 1649.

Several Passages in a Book printed, entituled, *A fiery flying Roll*, composed by one *Coppe*, were this day Read.

Resolved by the Parliament, That the Book entituled, *A fiery flying Roll, &c.* composed by one *Coppe*, doth contain in it many horrid Blasphemies, and damnable and detestable Opinions, to be abhorred by all good and godly people.

Ordered by the Parliament, That the Book entituled, *A fiery flying Roll, &c.* composed by one *Coppe*, and all the printed Copies thereof, be burnt by the hand of the Hangman, at the New Pallace-Yard at *Westminster*, the Exchange, in Cheapside, and at the Market-place in *Southwark*.

Ordered by the Parliament, That the Lord Major and Sheriffs of *London* and *Middlesex*, be enjoyned and required to take care that the same be done in the places aforesaid within their respective Liberties; And that the Bailey of *Southwark* be enjoyned and required to take care the same be done in *Southwark* accordingly.

Ordered by the Parliament, That the Sergeant at Arms do forthwith cause diligent search to be made in all places, where any of the said Blasphemous Books, entituled, *A fiery flying Roll, &c.* composed by one *Coppe*, are or may be suspected to be, and to seize them, and cause the same to be burnt at the places appointed; And that all persons who have any of the said Books in their custody, do cause the same to be burnt at the places aforesaid.

Ordered by the Parliament, That all Majors, Sheriffs and Iustices of Peace in the several Counties, Cities and Towns within this Commonwealth, be required to seize all the said Books in all places where they shall be found, and cause the same to be forthwith burnt by the hand of the publique Hangman.

Die Veneris, 1 Februarii, 1649.

ORdered by the Parliament, That these Orders be forthwith printed and published.

Hen: Scobell, Cleric. Parliamenti.

London, Printed by *Edward Husband* and *John Field*, Printers to the Parliament of *England*. 1649.

111

Aporia Press